D0065431

WORK
WITH
WHAT
YOU
GOT
25 IRON GRIP GYM
25 IRON GRIP GYM

WORK
WITH
WHAT
YOU
GOT
ZION CLARK AND JAMES S. HIRSCH

CANDLEWICK PRESS

Photo credits: p. i: copyright © 2023 by Oscar Garza; pp. ii–iii, v, viii, 2, 196, 212, 226: copyright © 2023 by Mada Abdelhamid/Real Deal; pp. 10, 18, 24, 30, 38, 48, 56, 62, 92, 100, 114, 156, 164, 190, 218: used with permission of Zion Clark; p. 74: used with permission of TSS Photography; pp. 84, 124, 144: copyright © ZUMA Press Inc./ Alamy Stock Photo; p. 134: used with permission of Kim Hawkins; p. 178: used with permission of Adaptive Sports Ohio

First edition 2023

Library of Congress Catalog Card Number 2022943165
ISBN 978-1-5362-2421-4

23 24 25 26 27 28 APS 10 9 8 7 6 5 4 3 2 1

Printed in Humen, Dongguan, China

This book was typeset in Scala.

Candlewick Press
99 Dover Street
Somerville, Massachusetts 02144

www.candlewick.com

A JUNIOR LIBRARY GUILD SELECTION

BE REAL.
BE YOU.

CONTENTS

WORK
WITH
WHAT
YOU
GOT

PREFACE

IF YOUR DREAMS DON'T SCARE YOU

I WALK INTO A ROOM and feel the stares. I take a few more steps, turn my head, and see it on their faces. Astonishment. Disbelief. A tinge of fear, perhaps. Some people approach me and introduce themselves. Others maintain their distance. A few others inch closer, peer, and retreat.

I am unlike anything they have ever seen.

I was born without legs, due to a rare medical condition known as caudal regression syndrome. I walk on my hands so that my arms are effectively my legs, yet I move as gracefully as anyone who has all four limbs, and with a six-foot-five wingspan, I can pull myself onto most any chair or platform and land like a hawk.

I am also young and Black.

Technically, I am disabled, and that's how the world sees me, but I have never defined myself that way. I'm just built lower to the ground. Besides, there is a difference between not having legs and believing you are missing something, and I can't miss what I've never had. So I adjust, improvise, and move on.

I used to be scrawny, but I have bulked up through weightlifting and can bench-press more than three hundred pounds—I've been called "Little Hercules." I can also do one-arm pull-ups from a high bar, dips with a heavy chain around my neck, and consecutive backflips like a circus performer. In 2021, I set a Guinness world record for being the fastest human on two hands after I ran twenty meters in 4.78 seconds. When I run, my arms move like two pistons that hurtle my body forward, and my undersized feet never touch the ground. Because I walk on my hands, they are covered with calluses so thick that I can scoop hot coals from a fire, toss them, and feel nothing.

I'm a professional athlete in the sport of wheelchair racing, but I have the body of a top-notch wrestler—which, in fact, I also am. I competed against able-bodied opponents in both high school and college and was involved in one of the most memorable high school wrestling matches in the history of Ohio. I continue to wrestle, and I also swim, dance, ride a bike, and drive my own car.

For me, every sport, indeed every activity, introduces unique challenges, which has led to a life of self-invention. Even simple tasks require creativity. I usually wear cutoffs, but I can't put too much in the pockets because they will drag along the ground. So I sometimes put the bottom of my T-shirt in my mouth and create a pouch—my friends call this my kangaroo style.

Another example: If an able-bodied person is packing his Xbox in a hotel room, he walks over to the desk, unplugs the video game, and carries it to his suitcase. Me? I walk across the room on my hands and then, using my arms as springs, leap onto the desk chair. Next, I pull myself up and stand on the desk, where I unplug the Xbox. Carrying it in one arm, I hop back onto the chair, using my free hand to grab the armrest, and then I jump to the ground, landing on my feet. These motions are done swiftly, nimbly, and seamlessly.

What is, for anyone else, a chair, a desk, or a bed is for me a series of navigational platforms. The physical world is my jungle gym.

Every disabled athlete has a story. To get on any field, court, or mat requires courage, perseverance, and the capacity to overcome self-doubt and defeat. Trust me; I know. I was so bad at wrestling for so many years that I could barely beat the wrestling dummies in practice. Disabled athletes make sacrifices that able-bodied athletes can only imagine, and that's okay. All anyone really needs to know about us is that we want to win just as badly as anyone else.

And we want to defy expectations. That's what motivates me. Tell me something I can't do, and I will do it, or die trying.

Or, as I tell kids:

NEVER GIVE UP, DREAM BIG,
AND BE THE PERSON YOU WERE BORN TO BE.

. . .

My story, however, is a little bit different than most "handicapped narratives." Actually, it's a lot different. Yes, I was born without legs and faced the dual stigma of being disabled and being Black, and sometimes I'm not sure which part of me the haters hate most. In another era, someone like me would have been isolated, abandoned, or discarded. That's what they did with "deformed kids." Eugenicists called people like me "subhuman."

But my disability and my race have not been the biggest challenges.

I was given up at birth by my mother, and I never met my father. I was put into the Ohio foster care system as a newborn, even though the system was never designed for a child like me. A foster home is supposed to be temporary until the child can reunite with family members, but I had no family. As a result, I spent my youth ricocheting from foster home to foster home, few of which seemed to really want me.

There are, to be sure, exceptional foster parents in Ohio and across the country, but overall, neglect is common. For years, I was so undernourished that my ribs protruded. For years, I was overmedicated on prescription drugs that were supposed to increase my focus but left me feeling dazed. I was often bullied and at times physically and emotionally abused, but even those assaults don't capture the full trauma of foster care. For the children, the system breeds a feeling of separation and detachment, of conditional acceptance. I always felt as if I were on trial. If I behaved well, I got to stay in the home. If I messed up, I was moved out. Spoiler alert: I was often moved out. At my lowest points, I considered suicide and even made some half-hearted attempts at it.

I found solace through books and music. I'm an accomplished trumpeter, keyboard player, and drummer, all self-taught, and I can play the ukulele, saxophone, and tuba. I was the lead trumpet in our marching band in high school. I'm a good artist as well. While I often struggled in school, I usually liked going because I knew I would be fed there. I feared going home because I didn't know what awaited me or whether I would be moved again.

What I know is that foster parents receive government money for each child they foster. In Ohio, it's about twenty-two dollars a day per child, but foster parents receive more money for a child with special needs—anywhere from forty to nearly two hundred dollars a day.

Strictly speaking, I was good business for the system.

I've received my share of media attention over the years. I was the subject of a short Netflix documentary, and I've been featured on ESPN and appeared on *The Ellen DeGeneres Show*. But all the media coverage glossed over the real story of my life. In the real story, I was labeled a "problem child," and for good reason. I *was* a problem child. But that's what happens when you grow up in a violent, unstable world.

I spent much of my youth in Massillon, Ohio, about sixty miles south of Cleveland. If the town is known for anything, it would be high school football, as it typically fields one of the best teams in the state. Football is the perfect identity for a community that was once part of a thriving industrial belt that produced coal, glass, and steel. Those days are gone, but the ethos of physical toughness remains, your character tested each day in the factories, sandlots, and streets. Those bare-knuckle expectations shaped me as a youth.

In my early teens, I lived in a bad part of town, and I ran with thugs who stole, brawled, broke into buildings, sold drugs, and flipped off cops. I did the same. Talk about an oddity: I was part of a street gang, which is pretty unusual for someone without legs, but it did have its advantages (we smuggled stolen goods from Walmart under my wheelchair seat). By seventeen, I had been arrested twice, once for assault. I've been cut with a switchblade and have had a gun pointed right in my face, but I never used a weapon to fight. I preferred my bare hands.

I got my life back on track thanks to a loving, pious woman who adopted me at seventeen and gave me what I never had before: a home, a mother, and a family. I also had a high school wrestling coach who never gave up on me and who pushed me to be the best wrestler, and man, I could be. Without my mom and my coach—and many others who refused to give up on me—I would have been another grim statistic of our nation's failed foster care system: homeless, incarcerated, or dead.

Finally, I give credit to God. Some of my earliest memories are of going to church—that's where I learned to play the drums—but I wasn't always a man of strong faith. However, watching my mom put faith into action had a huge influence on me, and I now carry a Bible wherever I go and recognize that every challenge has a purpose. Or as my mom often tells me, "God wouldn't take you through troubled waters if He knew you couldn't swim."

I'm still young, still a work in progress, but I've written this book with the hope that it will inform and inspire all who read it. I've learned that our greatest barriers are not physical. Our greatest barriers are those we impose on our own imaginations, ambitions, and dreams. Or, as a friend once told me,

**IF YOUR DREAMS DON'T SCARE YOU,
YOU AREN'T DREAMING BIG ENOUGH.**

CHAPTER 1
GRANNY'S LOVE

I WAS BORN IN COLUMBUS, Ohio, on September 29, 1997, to a woman who was in prison. I don't know if she was already pregnant when she was incarcerated or if she got pregnant after she arrived, though it doesn't really matter. She was a drug addict and also had diabetes, both of which apparently contributed to my birth defect. Caudal regression syndrome impairs the lower (caudal) end of the spine, and to call it rare is an understatement: it occurs in about one in twenty-five thousand live births, or 0.004 percent. Some people with this condition have less severe symptoms—reduced muscle mass in legs, clubfeet, webbed skin on the back of their knees. I got the version with no legs.

I have one toe on each undersized foot, but I don't have bone or nerves that connect my left foot to my hip, so I have no movement in that foot. It just sits there.

Otherwise, I was born physically normal.

I don't know if my birth mother gave me up because of my condition or because of her incarceration, though she did raise several other children. She also gave at least one other child away. Whatever the reason, she was never part of my life.

I wish I knew who my father was, but I don't.

My name at birth, Zion Zachariah Daniels, seems drawn from the Bible. Zion, in the Old Testament, is a mountain, which I take to mean sturdy. Preachers also refer to "the land of Zion," which I think is cool. Zechariah, in the New Testament, was a priest. My names seem to cover the Judeo-Christian waterfront.

My birth mother abandoning me was a blessing in the short term, as I was taken to Canton, Ohio, and placed in the foster home of a deeply religious and compassionate woman. We called her Granny, and I still call her that. She has broad shoulders and a soothing voice, and deep lines crease her face—the inevitable grooves, I feel certain, of her radiant smile, with which she greets every visitor. She has the rare power to make anyone in her presence feel comforted and cared for. I have few memories of my years living with her—I was too young—but my experience with her was important because it came to a terrible end. It was an early sign of the dysfunction and betrayal that awaited me in foster care.

Granny's name is Sarah Singleton, and she was born in rural Georgia during the Great Depression. Sarah lost her mother at age seven and was raised by her stern, God-fearing grandmother. She finished her schooling in seventh grade and was married at fifteen, after which she devoted herself to bearing and raising children. She had eleven of her own, though three did not survive, and she now has close to sixty grandchildren. "My whole life," she likes to say, "has been about kids."

She and her husband, a brick mason, moved to Pennsylvania when she was in her forties, and then she decided to separate because, as she tells me, "I was going to put some miles between me and him." She moved to Canton, where she had family, earned money cleaning offices, and settled into a modest two-story brick house with a small front yard.

This was the early 1980s, and one day while watching the news, Granny saw a story about children who needed foster homes until they could be reunited with their families. With her own kids grown, she thought she could do something for these children. She prayed on it and told the Lord, "I'm doing this for no money. I want to take care of these kids and give them back to their parents."

Stark County Job & Family Services conducted a background check and provided Granny with some training sessions, and she received her fostering license. The children started coming, and Granny's house became a haven for Black kids, though skin color made no difference to her. When a caseworker asked her if she'd be willing to take a white child, Granny told her: "Ma'am, a kid is a kid. Put a white one there and a Black one there, and you don't bother them, and that mama don't teach them any hatreds, and let them play, and they'll never know the difference. They're kids, and they just need someone to love them."

By 1997, she had fostered almost twenty children, and then in October of that year, a caseworker knocked on her door. She told Granny that she had a three-week-old baby boy whom the mother had given up and no one wanted. "You see," the caseworker said, "there is an issue. The baby is sweet, but he has no legs. Would you still be interested?"

Granny told her, "Even a baby with legs, what can he do? He'll be the same."

When the caseworker returned with me in a blanket, Granny needed no further convincing. As she tells me now, "You just took my heart away."

Granny always dressed me in nice clothes—I have the pictures to prove it—because she wanted me to look good. She was a working woman, mostly cleaning offices, and when she couldn't find someone to watch me, she took me with her and perched me on her buggy as she swept the floors and wiped down the bathrooms.

I was happy and rambunctious and enjoyed the two other foster children who were living with Granny—seven-year-old Ashley Hutchinson and her six-year-old brother, Travis. I was determined to follow them around, even if that meant some pratfalls. My head was too big for my body, so I would tip over while scampering about. Granny took me to doctors in Akron and Cleveland, and one of them strapped a bucket around my waist to help balance me. But I didn't like that bucket and ripped it off. Another doctor tried giving me prosthetics for my legs. They were supposed to help my spine, which has two metal rods in it, implanted when I was very young, because I had scoliosis, a curvature of the spine. But I hated the prosthetics and wouldn't wear them. And thus began my war against fake legs, which I would wage well into my high school years.

I taught myself how to walk using my arms, which made Granny both joyous and anxious. I was fearless! I'd hop onto the bunk beds or leap onto a couch. I felt stable and comfortable on my hands, but Granny thought I was taking too many risks.

"You can't do that!" she'd yell. "You're going to hurt yourself!"

"No, I'm not!" I'd shout back, and then I'd clamber along.

I taught myself how to go up and down stairs, and I climbed them faster than anyone with legs. When we went to the park, I'd chase the ducks or jump on the swings, and at home I'd do headstands or play with my Thomas train set. The first time I saw a kid ride a bike, I wanted that same bike. Granny told me I didn't have the legs for a bike, so she bought me a scooter that I powered by pumping the handles.

I also loved wrestling with the other boys in the neighborhood, even the ones who were a few years older, and Granny would say, "Careful, Zion! You don't have the strength!"

"Yes, I do!" I'd tell her.

When it was time to potty train me, she got me a little potty, lifted me onto it, and explained how to use it.

One day, I said, "Granny, I got to go to the bathroom."

"I'm coming," she said.

"I don't need you!"

"Zion, you don't have the means of getting up."

"Yes, I do! Watch me!"

She followed me into the bathroom, watched me lift myself up, and left.

She was too loving to be a true disciplinarian. One day, I was messing with an electric socket, which really scared her. She got her flyswatter and pretended like she was going to swat me, but I ran away. Then whenever I got out of line, she'd say, "I'm going to get my flyswatter!"

She never touched me, but I knew she was serious.

In her own way, she tried to prepare me for the world. One day at the park, for example, other children were teasing me.

"You don't have legs!" they yelled.

"Yes, I do!" I shouted. And I pulled up my shorts and showed them my two stumps with my tiny feet.

The teasing continued, and I went home crying.

There, Granny said to me, "You can do whatever you want to do, and you're just as good as anybody. I want you to fly."

When I think about the determination that I've had in life, I'm certain that Granny's encouragement at such a young age played a big role.

Granny also took me to Saint Mark's Baptist Church every Sunday, where congregants made me a blanket with biblical scenes and where I developed my initial interest in music. We sat in the pews during services and listened to the choir, accompanied by musicians, on the second level. When

I heard the drummer, I started tapping my hands on the back of the bench, in rhythm with the beat. So Granny took me to the drummer after the service. He was still at his drum set, and he put me on his lap, showed me how to hold the sticks, and—*Bang! Bang! Bang!*—I was hitting the snare. Granny was so impressed that she bought me a toy drum, which I pounded gleefully at home.

As my foster mom, Granny was supposed to care for me until I could reunite with my family, but I had no family, at least as defined by the state. It wasn't long before Granny began thinking about adopting me. She had not adopted any of her other foster children, and she wasn't thinking of adopting Ashley and Travis. We just had a special connection. I think she wanted to protect me as well. But then in July 1999, when I was almost two, the caseworker came to her house and told Granny that Ashley, Travis, and I were all going to be relocated 440 miles to upstate New York and placed in the home of another foster mom. The caseworker showed Granny pictures of a big house but didn't give her any explanation for why we were moving. Granny didn't understand but could do nothing about it. We were wards of the state. Foster care is temporary, and neither foster parent nor foster child has any say in the matter. And off we went.

CHAPTER 2
WHO'S GOING TO LISTEN TO A TEN-YEAR-OLD?

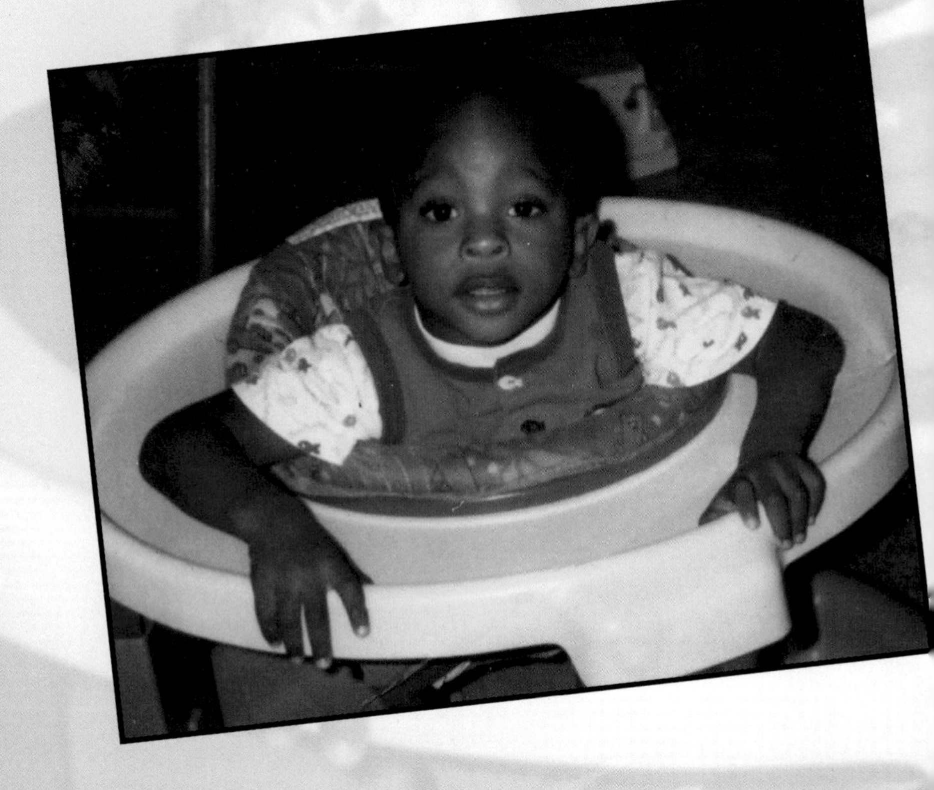

ASHLEY HAS ALWAYS BEEN a cheerful sort, with chubby cheeks, big black hair, and eyes that sparkle. She was nine when we were sent to Watertown, New York. I have no memory of the experience, but Ashley remembers it vividly and painfully, and she has shared it with me.

The foster mom in Watertown was a white physician who had several other foster children as well as an adopted son and a housekeeper. But we were the only Black kids in the house. The foster mom enrolled us in swimming classes and other activities, but she didn't understand that we came from a very different world. We had been going to a Black Baptist church, where we would whoop and holler, and she took us to her Catholic church, where we had to kneel and stay quiet. Granny always kept Ashley's hair real nice. Our new foster mom had no idea what to do with a Black girl's hair. She hired a Black woman to braid it, but she never got it right. Granny cooked us homemade meals. Our white foster mom served us Hot Pockets, canned green beans, and frozen foods.

It didn't take long before Ashley rebelled, and the tipping point was her radio: each day after school, she'd listen to her radio in her room. Then one day, to punish Ashley for not doing her chores, the foster mom took the radio away. Ashley called the foster mom a "white bitch," so the foster mom locked Ashley in her bedroom and boarded up the windows. The room also had an alarm, which Ashley intentionally set off. The woman threatened to beat Ashley, but Ashley said she'd kill her if she tried.

They were at war, but that was the least of it.

After we had been there nine months, the older adopted boy sexually assaulted Ashley. She was attending a Catholic school—she was its only Black student—and school officials noticed that her hair was disheveled, she hadn't bathed, and she was visibly distraught. They asked Ashley what happened, and she told them. She was sent to a hospital, where they administered a rape kit, and she was then taken to the police station, where she spoke to an investigator.

She was returned home, and in the days that followed, the older boy who was responsible had to leave the house under a restraining order, but Ashley, Travis, and I remained.

This was April 2000, the month Ashley turned ten.

Back at Stark County Job & Family Services, a new caseworker named Stephanie Carey had been on the job only a few months—she was still in training—when she was told to drive to Watertown, New York, with another trainee. There, she was to meet the sheriff, and they were to remove Travis, Ashley, and me from our home.

As Stephanie now tells me, Stark County officials had received reports that the house had older children who had been adopted, and these older children were "perpetrating" on the younger kids.

"Perpetrating" is their term for sexually inappropriate behavior or sexual assault.

According to the reports, because the foster mom in Watertown worked such long hours, the younger children lacked adequate supervision and were left to the mercy of these older kids.

Stephanie and her colleague drove to Watertown and, with the sheriff in tow, scooped up Ashley, Travis, and me and drove us back to Canton.

Ashley, at the time, didn't follow up with the authorities in Watertown or in Stark County—and how could she? This is one of the central problems of our foster care system: the only ones who really know what is happening to the foster kids are the kids themselves, but they don't have the authority to speak on their own behalf—particularly if their words cast the powers that be in a negative light. This happened to me so many times when I was in the system that I didn't believe I had a voice. Or as Ashley tells me about her experience, "Who's going to listen to a ten-year-old?"

. . .

Ashley is now in her early thirties, a mother herself, and she says she suffers from PTSD and anxiety from her trauma in Watertown. She wants accountability for what happened. In 2020, she called the investigator in Watertown with whom she'd spoken after the assault, and he remembered her. The detective also had a clear memory of me skittering along the floor when he entered the house—they hadn't had a report of a legless child—and he told Ashley that the basement looked like "a dungeon." One girl was locked in a cellar room, and the police had to snap the chain. Neither Ashley nor Travis knew anything about that. The investigator said that neither the foster mom nor her adopted son was ever charged with a crime.

After Ashley made her initial report, no investigator asked her any questions, and she was never asked to testify in court.

No one cared enough to do anything.

The whole incident was just swept under the rug.

The foster mother moved to another city, but she's easy to find on Facebook, and Ashley is not giving up. She is talking to the detective and seeking some measure of justice.

"I feel like we were sold to that lady, and we were there for nine months, and nobody ever came to check on us," she says.

There is one more question that burns in my mind: Why did anyone think it was a good idea to take three happy, well-adjusted Black children in Canton, Ohio, from a stable neighborhood with good schools, put them in a car, and move them to upstate New York?

I think I know. The foster mother was white. She had money. She lived in a big house. She may have promised Stark County officials that she would adopt us, which would have given us a permanent home. That's the objective. Find a permanent home to eliminate the transitions and instability of the foster system—but the authorities often don't do the research to find out what goes on inside that potential permanent home.

Ashley would ultimately live in seven different foster homes before she was adopted, becoming Ashley Charles. Travis was adopted by the same family. "Every foster child," Ashley tells me, "goes through abuse in foster care." Government agencies have created websites that show pictures of children who need to be adopted, and Ashley recalls sitting before a camera and doing video interviews to persuade someone to be her mother or father. "I felt like I was part of an auction," she says. "They would ask me, 'What is your dream?' My dream was to go to Disney World when I was adopted. I'm thirty-two years old, and I still haven't been to Disney World."

CHAPTER 3
UNDER THE RAINBOW

TRAVIS AND ASHLEY were delivered to another foster home in Canton, but I was returned to Granny and settled back into her house. At some point in 2001, she hired a lawyer to initiate her adoption of me. She wasn't expecting any problems—after all, she had raised me. But the process bogged down, as Stark County Job & Family Services, according to her, wouldn't give her my birth certificate or Social Security card. In October 2001, shortly after I turned four, the county authorities showed up at her house—and this is my first clear memory. I recall a caseworker putting me in a car and driving me away, and I remember entering a building with a rainbow over its front door.

A rainbow is supposed to be bright and happy, but at that moment, it was not happy to me. I cried and cried.

Granny had no idea why I was taken from her, but she and her daughter Rose followed the caseworker to Shipley Community Center on Second Street in Canton, which provides care to low-income families.

According to Granny, she and Rose were sent to one room, and I was in another, and they heard me screaming.

"I want my granny! I want my granny!"

Granny and Rose demanded to see me but were not allowed.

All they were told was that Granny would no longer be taking care of me—no fostering, no adoption, nothing.

Granny couldn't believe it. "Did I do anything wrong? Did I fail to take care of him?" she yelled out to the caseworkers, but received no response.

This broke her heart, both in its cruelty and in its arbitrary nature. She had done nothing wrong but was told the decision was final.

I was put back in a car and driven about eight miles west of Canton to the small town of Louisville (pronounced "Lewis-ville") and placed with Sandy and Ron Schmucker. I had been with them before on "respite," in which a foster parent leaves the child at another foster house for several days, and the foster parent is given a respite, or a break. Though I had been with the Schmuckers before, I yelled and screamed when I was dropped off, and I just sat down next to the front door and wouldn't move. I was inconsolable. And belligerent.

"Zion," Mrs. Schmucker said, "let's go into the other room. You know who we are."

"No! I want to go back to Granny. I want to go back to the rainbow room."

And I kept repeating that, over and over again.

"Well," Mrs. Schmucker said, "you can't do that right now. Maybe another day, but not right now."

I refused to go upstairs. I would have stayed there, next to the door, but Mrs. Schmucker finally picked me up, sat down in the rocker, and held me. "This is what we got to do," she said, "and this is what we're going to do."

She was with me all night, in the rocker. When the sun came up, she asked me, "Do you want breakfast?"

"No!"

"Oh, c'mon on. You're a growing boy. You have to eat."

I finally agreed, but I continued to ask if I could go to the rainbow room, and Mrs. Schmucker explained that I was going to have to stay with them for a while.

▪ ▪ ▪

Granny fought the decision that removed me from her home, and with the help of her lawyer, she had a court hearing, but her pleas did no good, and she lost her appeal. She doesn't know why she lost me, though it's possible the county just didn't believe a Black woman who cleans office buildings could create a permanent home for a child.

Granny knew one thing: she hadn't violated any rules or laws. If she had done anything wrong, she'd be in jail right now.

In time, an official from Job & Family Services knocked on Granny's door and asked if she would keep her beds open for other foster children.

"No, ma'am," Granny told her. "My heart goes out to all those children who come into the system. But you took my Zion from me. If you want to come back into my house, you'll bring Zion back."

I was Granny's last foster child, but that doesn't mean I was out of her life.

The foster community, in Stark County or anywhere else, is small, and Mrs. Schmucker knew Granny. She was not supposed to have any communication with her, but Mrs. Schmucker never really believed that the bureaucrats understood what foster kids went through. She had Granny's phone number in my paperwork, and she called her.

"Zion needs to see you," she said.

"But we aren't allowed," Granny told her.

"I know, but sometimes we go to McDonald's in Canton. Do you ever go to McDonald's in Canton?"

That's how I was able to occasionally visit Granny—not under the rainbow, but at least under the yellow arches.

CHAPTER 4
MY FEET ARE GROUNDED

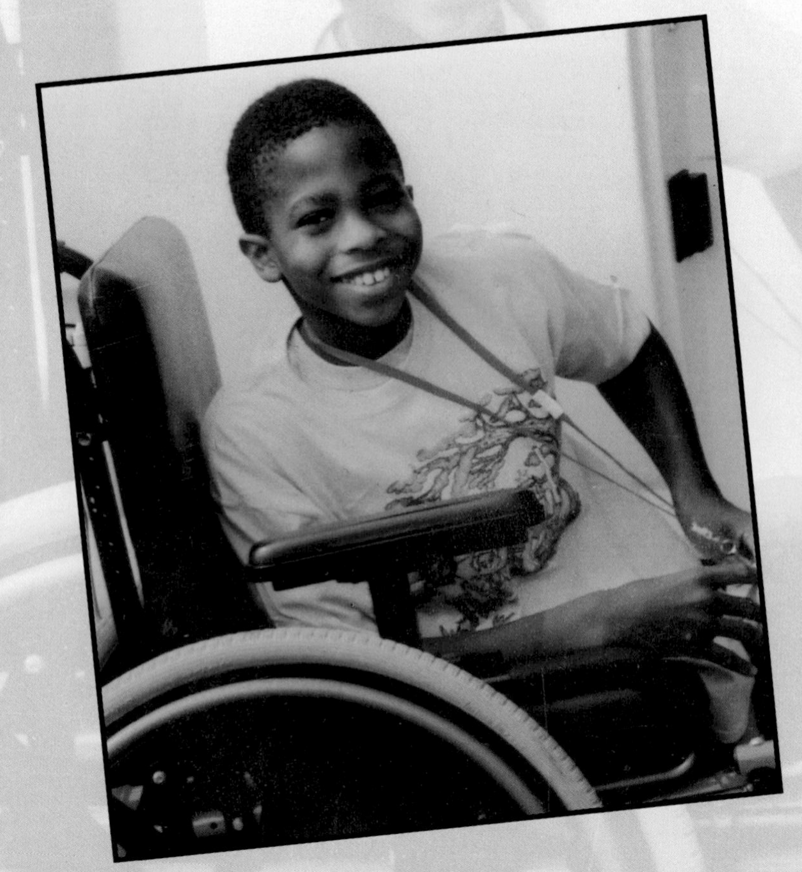

JUST AS GRANNY was a blessing in my life, so too were the Schmuckers, who were a periodic lifeline during my childhood and are two of the most exceptional people I've ever met.

Mrs. Schmucker had short, blondish hair, a stout build, and a ready smile. She just struck me as a happy woman. She had a loving grip when she picked me up, and she was one of the few people in my early years who could keep me calm. Mr. Schmucker was a bit thinner and older, with gray hair, a nice beard, and big brown glasses, and, like his wife, was a source of comfort. He always made sure I had what I needed. They both grew up in or around Louisville—Ron was one of fourteen siblings (yes, fourteen), which had taught him patience and made him a natural for the role that he and Sandy would play as a couple.

In 1968, they applied to Stark County to become foster parents, and two days later, a county official came to their home and handed Mrs. Schmucker a pink blanket. She took it, laid it on the couch, and asked, "Where's the baby?"

"I handed her to you," the official said.

"You did?"

She unfolded the blanket and found a tiny baby whose heart condition gave her a bluish tint. But the baby was a fighter and survived. When she was five years old, she had open-heart surgery, and she lived with the Schmuckers for twenty-six years.

The couple found their calling and decided to foster children with special needs. It didn't hurt that Mr. Schmucker was a respiratory therapist with a medical background, though nothing could prepare them for the challenges ahead.

One baby they fostered was born without a brain but lived off his brainstem. The caseworker told the Schmuckers that the child would probably only live a couple days.

"That's okay," Mrs. Schmucker said. "We don't ever count them out."

The Schmuckers cared for him for five years before he passed away.

In forty-eight years, the couple fostered more than a hundred kids, all with varying disabilities: children who were autistic, children who had cerebral palsy or who were born without limbs or with drug addictions, children who were born without health or hope. The most kids they could foster at one time, according to state law, was five. Regardless of how many children were living in their two-story home or what their disabilities were, either Sandy or Ron would stay up overnight in case of any medical emergency. They once hired an overnight nurse, but when she fell asleep on the job, they fired her.

When Stark County asked the Schmuckers to take in an able-bodied child, they said no. They were devoted to the children who needed them the most. There was the inevitable heartbreak—five children died when they were with the Schmuckers. But all were given a better life because of them.

Over the years, I lived with the Schmuckers about a half dozen times—either for respite or for longer stays when I was in between foster homes, for a total of twenty months over five years. They were the most consistent adult figures in my young life.

I was also the same kid with them that I was with Granny—as Mrs. Schmucker now tells me, instead of walking down the stairs one step at a time, I jumped five in one leap and scared the Schmuckers to no end.

"Zion, please don't do that," Mrs. Schmucker said.

"But it's fun!"

"I realize it's fun, but here's the problem. If you break your arms, how are you going to get around?" I had a wheelchair at that point, and she said I'd have to use it exclusively.

"No, I don't want to do that," I said. And I leaped down the stairs again.

I didn't care much for my wheelchair. I felt more natural

walking on my hands. When I was seven or eight, a boy down the street invited me to his birthday party. Mrs. Schmucker told me I could go by myself, but I had to take my wheelchair. She was afraid drivers wouldn't see me if I was just walking on my hands. So I rode the chair to the end of the Schmuckers' driveway, got out, and walked the rest of way. After the party, I walked back to the driveway—but the wheelchair was gone! I was in big trouble.

I went inside and told Mrs. Schmucker what had happened.

"Well," she said, "someone must have taken it."

I was really shaken, but then I saw the glint in her eye.

She told me that she saw the chair on the driveway and brought it inside. But she was disappointed in me.

"Why didn't you just tell me you didn't want to use your wheelchair?" she asked.

"I wanted to walk on my hands."

"I thought you'd be safer in your chair," she said, "but I would have let you."

We would have similar arguments at the grocery store. I wanted to walk on my own, but Mrs. Schmucker wanted me to ride in the cart, because she was concerned that someone would step on me.

Otherwise, the Schmuckers often gave me some free rein. They were fine when I rode my skateboard down the sidewalk. They didn't like it, though, when I played football with the other kids. They were afraid I would break an arm, which for me would also mean breaking a leg. I played anyway. I also loved playing kickball, using my arm as my leg to slam the ball into the outfield and over the heads of the other kids. Even though I was gaunt, my arms were deceptively strong because I walked on them every day—just moving around, in effect, was a day at the gym.

It all seemed very normal to me, and when I was young, I didn't really appreciate my complete otherness unless someone mentioned it. That happened when Mrs. Schmucker enrolled me in first grade at Louisville Elementary School.

"You'll be the only Black child in an all-white world," she told me.

I would also be the only child without legs, but I guess she figured she didn't need to tell me that.

When we were walking down the hall, some kids stared at me, aghast. One said, "Look at that poor kid. Do you think he got hit by a train?"

Mrs. Schmucker leaned toward me and said, "Zion, did you hear what that kid said about you?"

"Yeah," I said. "Why didn't you tell him I didn't get hit by a train?"

"Next time," she said, "you tell me when you want me to say something like that."

I now understand that she wanted me to advocate for myself at a young age, and not just with other kids. I had to learn to advocate for my own health. In addition to the two metal rods implanted in my back, I had also had an operation on my stomach as a young child. I have no memory of it, but it's in my medical file. I also had to see an intestinal doctor, a bladder doctor, a spine doctor—all kinds of doctors for all kinds of problems.

Then there were my feet. I've received my share of disparaging remarks about them, and it's not an accident that my pant legs cover them. My feet are what they are. Undersized. One toe on each. No movement in my left. But I can control the movement in my right foot and my right toe, which is really helpful when I wrestle, as I can use that foot—specifically my right toe—to maneuver and launch. No one's right toe is as important to them as mine is to me. I cannot stand on my feet without the help of my arms (or to be more precise, I can stand on my left arm and my right leg).

I tried putting socks on my feet, but they rarely stayed on. Both of my feet dangle, and they get caught in rugs, in regular doors, in car doors, and in elevator doors. That's painful. The nails on my two toes are shaped kind of weird, so that also complicates moving on certain types of floors or fabrics.

All these problems were evident at a young age, and Mrs. Schmucker was apparently the first person to take me to a doctor about my feet. I was three or four at the time, and the doctor recommended amputating both my feet. Just cut them off. Useless.

Mrs. Schmucker said I used my right toe to balance myself.

"Let's take off the left foot then, since it serves no purpose," the doctor said.

"Zion will make that choice for himself when he gets older," Mrs. Schmucker told him.

That's what made Mr. and Mrs. Schmucker so special. Despite my otherness, they knew I was like any other kid. They knew I was capable and, when old enough, I could make life-changing decisions on my own.

By the time I was a teenager, I started having my own discussions with doctors about my feet and whether they should be amputated. I didn't want to because I would need about a year to heal—which meant no wrestling—and I would have to reinvent how to balance myself and how to move around. When I retire from sports, I might have my left foot removed and replaced with a fake foot that doesn't cause me discomfort. But I'm keeping my right foot.

CHAPTER 5
NO WAY TO RAISE A KID

I WAS FORTUNATE to have two early foster homes—Granny's and the Schmuckers'—that were so good. It wasn't usually like that for me, and it's not like that for most foster kids in Stark County or anywhere else.

As of this writing, the county has 120 licensed foster homes to care for about 360 kids. Private agencies also place foster kids. To be certified, a foster parent must be at least twenty-one, complete at least thirty-eight hours of training, pass a criminal background check, and be recertified every two years.

The goal of the foster system is to provide a temporary home until a permanent home, known as a "forever family," can be found. Ideally, this forever family would be with the child's biological parents or with another family member: a "kinship caregiver," as they term it. If those options are not available, then the child will typically bounce from one foster home to the next, until a foster parent adopts that child.

Even if the system worked perfectly, its limitations are easy to identify. Foster care's overriding objective is to reunite the child with a biological parent or to place the child in a permanent home. But what about the child who has no family to return to or whose biological parents are deemed unfit? The system wasn't built for that child.

Foster parents may love a foster child, but if they have no interest in adoption—in making a forever family—then that child will be moved to another home, creating yet another loss for the child. Then there is the loving foster parent who wants to keep the child but loses that child to the biological parent who is now deemed fit. Once again, the child is on the move. Then there are the respites, which may indeed give foster parents a much-needed break, but they also require moving children from one home to the next. However brief, respites are another disruption for the child.

Even in ideal scenarios, in which foster parents are well trained, the foster homes are stable, and the caseworkers are vigilant, the foster child experiences physical and emotional whiplash. I've seen it; I've experienced it.

Because I had no kinship family, the authorities (first Stark County, then later a private agency) always tried to place me with foster parents who expressed interest in adopting me. But Stephanie Carey, who picked me up from Watertown and was my caseworker until I was nine, recognized how unprepared many would-be adoptive parents were. As she tells me now, too many of these adults would scroll through the website of adorable children and fall in love with the photograph. (My picture was only from the waist up.) Then these adults would have a trial weekend or a full week with the child, and they'd go to an amusement park and a ball game and McDonald's and would have all kinds of fun, and everyone was happy. So the child would join the family, but then reality would set in. And guess what? Parenting is a lot more complicated than amusement parks and ball games and McDonald's.

Stephanie conducted a training exercise for parents who were thinking about adoption. She instructed them to draw a stick figure of the child that they wanted to adopt, and that picture represented their perfect child in all his or her beauty and potential. Stephanie then asked the parents to hand her the picture, whereupon she ripped it into shreds. She handed one piece back to each parent.

"This," she said, "is the child you're getting."

Just one piece, and no more. It was her dramatic way of saying that the child had already been through tremendous loss and grief and that the child could not possibly be whole.

But according to Stephanie, this lesson rarely stuck. "The parents saw what they wanted to see," she says. "They saw the perfect kid. They didn't see or acknowledge all of the losses, all of the heartbreak."

She doesn't blame the caseworkers, who for the most part, she says, are overworked. But the system doesn't properly identify, and then train, qualified foster and adoptive parents, particularly for disabled children.

Sandy Schmucker saw how often those children were abused. In one instance, she and her husband fostered a child who was autistic—"a darling boy," she says—until the authorities found him a potential forever home with parents interested in adoption. Disaster followed. The boy was severely abused at that house, and the authorities returned him to the Schmuckers. "He came back a totally different child," Mrs. Schmucker says. "When he was here, he talked, ate by himself, walked around. When he came back, he couldn't do any of that."

She says that the higher payments for fostering or adopting disabled children can lure the wrong type of parents, but disabled children are more vulnerable to abuse simply because of their disability.

"The authorities don't pay as much attention to them because, in some cases, they can't talk and can't tell you what's going on inside the home," she said. "For the child who can't communicate as well, the caseworker says, 'They've got clothes, they're being fed, they're fine.' Any child who looks weak will be taken advantage of. I really do believe that."

Granny was the last Black foster parent I lived with until I was fourteen. I'm not saying a white parent can't raise a Black child. All a kid wants, really, is security and to know that he is part of the family. That can happen regardless of race, ethnicity, or religion. But a white parent raising a Black child doesn't make it any easier, and it certainly didn't for me.

Whenever I'd go into a new home, things would usually start out well, and the family would tell me how much they wanted me to be there. I think most foster parents believe that at the beginning. The problem is that every kid makes mistakes or does something wrong or stupid, so being a good parent requires patience and commitment, and my foster parents didn't necessarily have that, particularly if they had two, five, or ten other kids (foster, biological, step-) in the same house.

And sometimes the other kids can be worse than the parents.

When I was six years old, I lived with a foster family in North Canton, and I honestly don't know why the parents wanted me. I once left a piece of Laffy Taffy in my pants pocket. The candy attracted ants, which found their way into the prosthetics I was wearing at the time, and my foster parents still made me wear them, with the crawling bugs, to teach me to be more careful. When I cried, they beat my butt so hard that I'm pretty sure I still have scars. At other times, they would punish me by making me sit in the corner and telling me to keep my arms up until they hurt.

But that was not the worst part. It was in that house that an older foster boy came into my bedroom one night and touched me inappropriately. Afterward, he told me that if I let anyone know, he'd kill me. I was scared. I didn't tell my foster parents because I knew they wouldn't believe me, but after a while, I did tell a counselor at school. The counselor notified someone with the county, and I was removed from the house, but it took a couple months.

I assume there were no consequences for anyone, but I still have nightmares about what happened. It's not something you easily forget, no matter how young you are when it happens, and sometimes the memories can kill my vibe with a woman. I don't talk about it, and it's not easy to share in these pages, but I am sharing it because it's important that other victims know they are not to blame and they should do everything possible to seek help.

After that incident, I was taken to the Schmuckers' house for eight months, sent to another foster home for eight more months, then moved back in with the Schmuckers for three months, and then shipped to North Canton to another home. I was eight years old.

I now understand that these upheavals—moving from house to house, combined with neglect and abuse—changed me. They made me less trusting, more introverted, more impulsive, and angrier. When I would get angry, I'd lose control and throw fits—and sometimes objects. Or I'd pull things off of walls. I've also always had a hard time staying focused and was later diagnosed with ADHD, or attention deficit hyperactivity disorder. I'm not blaming all of these issues on foster care. I am saying it's no way to raise a kid.

In North Canton, I moved in with a single mother who actually adopted me and gave me her last name. She was a gym teacher at a school for children with special needs. She had a biological son and daughter who were both older than I. Finally, a permanent home! You'd think she'd be well suited to take care of a child like me, but she wasn't.

For example, I attended Orchard Hill Intermediate School, and in second grade, we had Pajama Day. I wanted to go in my pajama bottoms, but my mom said no. I put them on anyway, and my mom called me an idiot and threw a chair at me. I went on the bus, my face bleeding, and the bus monitor, a sweet Black woman named Debbie McGuire, cleaned me up. She took me to the office, and one of the school administrators called my mom, who denied that she'd done anything to me. When I got back home, she grounded me. I still have a faint scar on my nose from the chair.

On another occasion, I wanted to dress up as Darth Vader for Halloween, but my mom refused to get me a costume. I went trick-or-treating anyway but had to give my candy to my brother. I've hated Halloween ever since.

Maybe I was just too unusual to fit into my mom's idea of family. One day in fourth grade, I was wearing my prosthetics and was also in my wheelchair, and when I leaned over to pick up my pencil, one of my fake legs snapped and broke. When my mom picked me up, she screamed at me for breaking the leg. We had to go to the doctor to get it fixed.

My mom decided to take me to an anger management class in Cleveland, where I met a counselor once a week. My mom told the counselor I did all kinds of things that I never did, such as beat the dog. I love animals and would never hurt a dog. I always felt that I entered those counseling sessions as the accused party, and even as a third grader, I had to defend myself. In retrospect, I believe that my adopted mom was just trying to blame me for her failures as a parent.

I was with this family for about two years, and one day my mom dropped me off at respite, which is available for adoptive parents as well. I assumed I'd be there for two or three days, but my mom never came back. That was that. She dropped me off and abandoned me, without even saying goodbye. Even though she had adopted me, she did whatever she had to do legally to sever ties. All she left me with was her last name, and I was once again without a family, so I was returned to the foster care system.

But at least one good thing happened during those years in North Canton. In second grade, I had an amazing art teacher named Greg Donahue. He taught me how to make a cat out of Styrofoam, using a pencil to make strategic indentations.

"That's a nice cat," he told me when I was finished.

I wasn't used to getting compliments, so that meant a lot.

Mr. Donahue was lean and athletic, and one day he walked

up to me and said, “You look like a wrestler.” He handed me a flyer for a local wrestling league.

I thought he meant WWE, and I envisioned jumping off a rope and giving someone an elbow, which sounded fun.

I took the flyer home and asked my mom if I could wrestle. She agreed, and I joined the wrestling league. At my first practice, I quickly realized that this wasn’t WWE—I couldn’t just jump on a kid. This was real wrestling. But because I was so small and so unfamiliar with all the moves—and the moves themselves, for the most part, required legs—I wasn’t any good. Nevertheless, thanks to Mr. Donahue, my wrestling career had begun.

CHAPTER 6
FINDING MY SUPERPOWERS

WHEN I THINK about my childhood, what I most remember is how hungry I always was. Whether it was pushing my wheelchair or walking on my hands, I was burning calories nonstop, and until I started lifting weights in high school, I was so skinny you could see my rib cage. Some of the homes I lived in withheld food for discipline. If I did something wrong, I was denied dinner, or even dinner and breakfast, or in extreme cases, all three meals. Sometimes my rations were reduced, or I would only get to drink milk. I often wasn't allowed to watch TV or play video games, and to this day, I still don't do much of either. I never had many friends. I read a lot, which, bizarrely, once got me in trouble.

In fourth grade, I was sent to a house in Perry, next to Massillon, for respite. There, I brought home a Harry Potter book, and the mom screamed at me. She was a devout Christian, and she thought the book was inspired by the devil. I still read it, which got me grounded.

But reading was a huge part of my youth: books were safe, and they removed me from my reality. Fantasy fiction was my favorite, and I loved the characters who went on heroic journeys. I read the *Lord of the Rings,* and my favorite character was Frodo, whose quest requires him to take the One Ring to Mount Doom and destroy it, and even though Frodo is wounded, he succeeds and gains wisdom along the way.

I felt an even closer connection to Percy Jackson, the hero in Rick Riordan's Heroes of Olympus series. Percy is a dyslexic, hyperactive kid who struggles in his classes and is repeatedly kicked out of school. His father abandoned him before he was born, and Percy resents him for his neglect. But he soon discovers that his father is one of the Olympians, Poseidon, making Percy the son of the sea god—half human, half immortal—and beyond the comprehension of any normal being. Percy is sent on dangerous quests to save the world. His superpowers allow him to escape a fire-breathing Chimera at the top of the Gateway Arch by jumping into the Mississippi River. He commands ocean waves to engulf homicidal gods, makes himself invisible to evade the Furies, and uses his magical bronze sword to conquer monsters, beasts, and winged predators.

Percy triumphs. He becomes a hero. Yet he remains humble and vulnerable because, I think, he knows he doesn't really fit into the Olympian world.

He eventually meets his father, who acknowledges these burdens.

His father tells him that he is sorry Percy was ever born and explains that he has brought Percy "a hero's fate," which is "never anything but tragic."

But Percy accepts his unwanted role—he embraces the

tragedy of his own life—and simply says, "I don't mind, Father."

Percy is twelve years old.

I couldn't jump off the Arch or create tsunamis in the ocean, but Percy was the hero that I wanted to be—the abandoned, misunderstood swashbuckler who avenges the wrongs of the world.

I also read Kyle Maynard's memoir, *No Excuses: The True Story of a Congenital Amputee Who Became a Champion in Wrestling and in Life*. It's an adult book, but I read it when I was eight. Kyle was born with shortened arms and legs, but he became a top high school wrestler. He describes how, supported by a loving family, he succeeded as both a young athlete and a person. Mr. Donahue gave me the book. I didn't have any role models when I was young because I couldn't identify with anyone. But I could with Kyle.

Because I read so much, I would devour books straight through and always read at a higher grade level than the one I was in. I had a better vocabulary than my peers and was always confident as a speaker. When I was eighteen or nineteen and suddenly found myself on television as a result of a documentary made about me, I was never that nervous because I felt my command of language was strong. That's the benefit of reading so much.

But just because I was a good speaker doesn't mean I did

a lot of talking in class or in groups. I was more apt to sulk than speak. It was my way of protesting.

Ever since I was young, people have underestimated my intelligence. I was sent to Eastgate Early Childhood and Family Center, a preschool for kids who have learning or developmental disabilities or who are on the autism spectrum. It's important that such a school exists for those kids, but I didn't have a learning or developmental disability, and I wasn't on the spectrum. They eventually figured that out and put me in a regular school. Throughout my youth and even to this day, people will bend down and speak to me slowly—as if their words, literally and figuratively, will go over my head. Many white people underestimate the intelligence of young Black men. That's based on racial biases that are deeply embedded in our country's history, and for those of us who are young and Black, it comes with the territory. But the perception that a person without legs is somehow impaired mentally is—at least in my case—a second insult, and it motivates me even more to defy expectations.

My music is a good example.

The drums were my first instrument, and I learned to hold the sticks at Granny's church, but for the most part, my drum playing has been entirely self-taught. Granny bought me the toy drum, and I would also bang pots and pans. But when I was eight, I got a beginner's drum set—a snare, a tom-tom, a bass, and a high hat, a pair of cymbals operated by a foot pedal. The set was easy to assemble, which I did in the basement, but that didn't mean I could play it. It had foot pedals to hit the bass drum as well as the high hat, but my feet didn't reach the pedals. My drumming career almost came to an end before it started, but I really wanted to play those drums. So I made prongs long enough to reach the foot pedals and attached them to the bottom of my stool. By shifting my weight to the right or left, I could make the prongs hit the pedal for the bass or the cymbal.

That's when I first started thinking: **WORK WITH WHAT YOU GOT.**

Once I figured out how to play my drums, I shut the basement door and used my CD player and headphones to listen to songs and then bang out the beat. My favorite song was "Rock Steady," by a Christian children's rock band called God Rocks! "Rock Steady" has an amazing beat and connects faith to music.

I put my CD player on repeat and played that song over and over, and it was then that I realized I could be a good drummer. It was like the universe was speaking to me through those headphones. I kept thinking, *Playing the drums is your thing, man, and no matter where you're at or what you're going through, music is going to save you.*

I didn't stop with the drums. Not long after I got my first drum set, I stayed with the Schmuckers for several weeks. They had a keyboard in the house, which they let me tinker with. But I didn't want to just tinker. I wanted to play it. So at school, I used a computer to learn bass and treble clef notes. I'd listen to songs on a small radio, and once I found the bass note at the start of the song, I could play the rest.

When I was in fifth grade, three years after I began playing the drums and the keyboard, I started playing the trumpet. I thought it looked cool, and I wanted to try it, so I joined the school band. We were seated by ability. I started out fifth chair among the other trumpeters, but I went home and practiced every day. I didn't take any lessons but just played by myself. To challenge the next chair, I had to memorize my scales, hit the higher notes, and play progressions. In just one school year, I became the first chair; by sixth grade, I was playing at a tenth-grade level; in high school, I was good enough to join a band that played in bars on jazz night.

I loved playing music because it allowed me to drift off into some other space, and it put me at peace. I loved it because no one could tell me what to do with it. And I loved it because it was mine.

My life has been all about persistence and reinvention. Though Granny wouldn't let me ride a bike, I still wanted to, and when I was in second grade, my adoptive mom bought me a bike with a hand crank. I wanted nothing to do with that bike. I wanted a bike like the other kids had. My mom finally got me a blue one with training wheels. I didn't like that one, either, because most second graders don't need training wheels. That blue bike just sat in the garage. I took it with me, however, to my next home, and when I was in fourth grade, I saw all these kids riding their bikes, and I asked, Why can't I? So I got my bike, took off the training wheels, and tried to teach myself to ride. I fell off more times than I can count, but I figured it out. I put my left arm across the handlebars and my right hand on the right pedal. I've always had long arms, and here they were a big help. I teetered, I balanced, I pumped the pedal, I shot forward, and suddenly I was really moving! I was riding my bike. It was all about maintaining balance.

These were not the superpowers of my heroes, but they were *my* superpowers, and they worked for me.

I can now ride any bike, but I draw the line at unicycles.

CHAPTER 7
MY FIRST FRIEND

I MOVED TO MASSILLON at the start of fifth grade, which was the first year of Massillon Junior High School. New family. New town. New school. As always, a lot of change. I later discovered that I was placed with this new family by a private agency, Pathway Caring for Children, instead of by Stark County. The county typically uses a private agency when it cannot find a suitable home within its own network, and I assume that's what happened to me.

My new foster home had eight or nine other kids, foster and biological combined, as well as seven Chihuahuas, four cats, and two birds. My home life, initially, was relatively stable (if crowded), but school was more challenging.

I always knew when kids were staring at me, and the taunts were inevitable. They called me "mutant" and later, in high school, "Lieutenant Dan," after the Vietnam veteran in *Forrest Gump* who lost his legs in battle. Even though I was puny, I was never one to back down. But as I got older, I became sensitive to the slights and more willing not only to fight back but to escalate. That's how we settled things. You get challenged, you fight back. I was always underestimated.

Because I couldn't maneuver like everyone else, and because I was so small, kids thought they could just kick me over. But even when I was in elementary or middle school, I had strength in my arms and hands. When a kid would run at me full speed and kick one leg toward my face, I'd grab it with one hand and use my other hand to sweep his other leg out from under him. He'd end up on the ground, I'd be on top, and I'd make him pay.

I had plenty of these battles in middle school, and I lost my share. But I kept fighting. Then something important happened in sixth grade. I made my first friend. Until I met Kelcey Leonard, I always felt isolated, whether I was in my home or at school. I'm not sure any of the other kids who knew me wanted to be my friend, and I'm not sure I wanted to be theirs. And frankly, I wasn't looking for a friend on the day I met Kelcey.

We were put at the same table because we had failed to do our homework, so I guess we had that in common. She was white, lanky, with reddish-brown hair, and on the day we met, she saw a kid in our class bully me, calling me names, making fun of my disability, and she challenged him. "What are you gonna do about it?" he said.

This was routine for me, but Kelcey was outraged. She was also taller than the kid and told him to get lost, which he did. But later she went home crying and told her mom what had happened.

"They're making fun of him," Kelcey said. "He just doesn't have legs."

She came back to school the next day, and we started hanging out. She was always kind, she didn't care what other people thought, and she was brutally honest.

She didn't live with her father, and the whole absent-father plight was one of many things that we had in common. Like me, Kelcey also had a hard time keeping friends. We're both high-strung and righteous, and sometimes we can even be too much for each other. But Kelcey has a soft spot for outcasts. Whenever someone talked bad about me behind my back, she spoke up. Whenever someone tried to bully me, she protected me. Whenever I got angry, I called her, and she'd tell me that I had to be the bigger person. And I was a good friend right back. When her best friend's mother died, I helped her through it. At another point, Kelcey was hospitalized for several days, and I was right there with her, holding her hand, telling her she'd be fine. She would have done the same for me. I even helped her pick out her dress for our senior prom, a strapless yellow-gold ensemble. She tells me that when she gets married, I can help her choose her wedding gown.

I often wondered why some kids treated me like a regular kid while many others didn't. In Kelcey's case, I think it was because of her mom, Stefanie, who was also a big part of my childhood. Stefanie always carried herself with such strength and confidence, and she and Kelcey looked so much alike—the same blue eyes, thin lips, beautiful face. They welcomed me into their lives as if I were a family member. They didn't care about community expectations or what it might look like to have a white family embrace a Black kid without legs. Norms didn't matter. But life did—and Stefanie had her own life experiences, I think, that made her sensitive to mine.

She was born and raised in Massillon but moved around as a kid. She lived mostly with her mother, who, as she tells me, "just moved to wherever the guy she dated was." Stefanie failed third grade because she missed so many classes. In high school, she took machine trades so she could find a good job, but when she was a sophomore, she got pregnant. The father was a freshman football player. After Kelcey was born, Stefanie and the baby received food stamps, and after Stefanie graduated high school, she and Kelcey moved into an apartment in Massillon, with Stefanie working as a machine apprentice. Kelcey's father was never a big part of her life.

Stefanie's family grew, as she had two boys with another man whom she didn't marry. She worked midnight shifts to try to make ends meet. So growing up, Kelcey had a very young, single working mother whom she helped in raising the two little boys, her brothers, Karson and Kyler. Stefanie eventually quit her industrial job to spend more time with her kids, and she earned money babysitting, bartending, and ultimately by founding a successful business baking and decorating cakes from her kitchen.

All of this affected my life. Stefanie now spent most of her days and nights at home, allowing me to be a bigger part of their family. Kelcey played the flute, so her mother would pick us from band practice, drive us around town, and invite me to their house. I would also show up on my own at all hours. I loved playing with Karson and Kyler, who liked to wrestle, and of course I loved the fresh-baked cakes. Stefanie always fed me, which was important, because for much of my life, I was often hungry.

Only later did I learn that Stefanie wanted to adopt me. She didn't because she assumed that as a single parent, she would have been rejected. Regardless, I had more reason than usual to be grateful that I met Kelcey and her mom when I did. They came along at one of the worst times in my life.

CHAPTER 8
DROWNING

I ALWAYS TRIED to keep my home life separate from my school life, and both separate from my social life. Some overlap was inevitable, but I had so many stress points that I thought keeping everything separate was better. Both Kelcey and her mom, however, knew that the home in Massillon, where I was placed in fifth grade, wasn't good. The warning signs were obvious.

The reason Kelsey's mom had to drive me everywhere was that my foster parents wouldn't pick me up from school or take me to band practice or attend my wrestling matches. When Kelcey's mom couldn't drive me after school, I would push my wheelchair several miles home. In the mornings, my foster parents would drive their other kids to school but make me take the bus. I didn't ask why; if I had, they would have yelled at me.

My friendship with Kelcey was a whole other problem. My foster parents didn't like her and wouldn't let me see her, which meant she couldn't come over to the house. My foster parents also took away my phone just so I couldn't call Kelcey.

But their disdain for her made no sense. My foster parents were white, so maybe they opposed interracial friendships.

The house was so crowded with kids and animals, no single kid was going to get that much attention. Many foster kids just learn how to survive in whatever environment they're in, and interestingly enough, that's how I learned to swim.

This foster home had a swimming pool, and one day one of the older boys said, "You're going to learn how to swim now." He threw me into the pool, and I sank to the bottom. I assume someone would have pulled me out had I not resurfaced. I thrashed upward and got my head above water.

The boy who threw me in began to mimic the freestyle stroke. "Move your arms like this!" he yelled.

I had been to swim meets and knew what the stroke looked like. But seeing it and doing it are two different things. Now here I was, gasping for air, flailing, with others looking on in amusement. Sink or swim, indeed. I tilted my body forward, put my head down, and pounded the water with my arms. I wasn't graceful, or proud. But the length and strength of my arms allowed me to stay afloat and propel forward.

I survived my maiden voyage into the water, and I enjoy swimming on a hot day, though it's not really a recreational activity for me. Unless I'm in a kids' pool or the shallow end, I can't stand up, and I don't have all the parts to be a fast swimmer. But I developed my own plow-forward style, which I'll call the don't-give-in-to-these-bastards-who-don't-think-you-can-swim stroke.

Other times at this house, I did feel like I was drowning.

I had recently been diagnosed with ADHD, mainly because I had trouble staying focused at school. And I was put on not one, but two different medications—Adderall and Vyvanse. I took them every day. Both are stimulants that were supposed to sharpen my focus and decrease my impulsiveness, and I believe these drugs did help me in the classroom. I was calmer. But the drugs often left me numb. There were times, mainly in class, when I just sat there, didn't talk, and was almost in a trance. I knew the drugs were doing that to me, but I never asked to stop taking them. I was developing a dependency on them and was scared what would happen if I stopped.

The meds didn't change how I was seen by my foster parents. As I later discovered, the caseworker file that went to all my foster parents identified me as a problem kid. The Schmuckers never paid attention to the file or to what others said about me, because they made the effort to understand who I was and what I was going through. But the other foster parents simply saw me as that problem kid, and this was certainly true with the foster parents who put me on the meds.

That's why, I believe, they wouldn't take me to the movies

with their other kids (foster and biological) or let me play video games. I had to take short showers and clean up dog poop and scrub the bathrooms. If I got in trouble, I was denied TV or food (when everyone got pizza, I got cereal) and was grounded for two months at a time. All the kids in the house got iPod Touches for their birthdays. I didn't get anything. Whenever I complained, they always threatened to get rid of me, and that was the worst part. They always made me feel as if I wasn't worthy and that I didn't belong.

The meds didn't muddle my thinking about how I saw the world. I thought it was cruel and we were all just survivors in it, which is a lot for a kid in middle school to absorb. The meds also didn't make me a better or a different kid. I got my first detention in seventh grade, one of many that year, and my grades plunged. I was getting into fights at the slightest provocation. I was so depressed that I thought about suicide and one time even pondered how I could use a belt to hang myself.

I was still going to my anger management class, but it wasn't going any better. In a typical session, the counselor asked me why I was angry.

I told her because I hated everybody.

She asked me why.

I told her because I was getting bullied.

She had some suggestions. She told me to smile at my tormentors and walk away. She encouraged me to focus on other things—reading, wrestling, playing cards, expressing myself artistically. I did a lot more drawing and loved sketching dope-ass dragons, animals, and superheroes. Superman battling Batman was always fun, or Goku from the Dragon Ball manga series. Goku was a boy who practiced martial arts and grew up to become the world's mightiest warrior.

These artistic diversions were good for me, and I recognize that the counselor gave me sound advice. But I still never made a strong connection with her. She also saw me as a problem kid, and there was nothing I could say or do to change that.

At some point in middle school, my foster parents stopped taking me to the counselor. I guess they didn't see the value in it and didn't like driving to Cleveland. I still have an anger streak, but it's much harder to trigger and I channel it more productively.

Growing up, I was told by my caseworkers that my biological mom had several other children, but I didn't know them. Then when I was twelve, my caseworker told me that I had a biological brother who was eight years younger, and he wanted to see me. Arrangements would be made through my foster parents.

His name was Samuel, and he lived in Alliance with his adoptive mother. My whole life, I had seen kids who had brothers and sisters as well as parents, grandparents, and cousins. Every family has its own history, and that history grounds its members in its own narrative and connects them to one another. I was lonely, I think, in part because I didn't have that narrative and didn't have those connections. Now I had a brother! I couldn't wait to see him.

We met at a McDonald's in Canton, and the first thing I noticed was how similar we looked. Same eyes, same nose, same lips, same upper body. He was like my younger twin, except he had legs.

I showed him and his mom, Shannon Kerr, some of my drawings of birds. Samuel was sweet and gentle but wasn't that talkative. I could tell by his expressions, however, that he was happy to be there and to have a big brother he was related to by blood. (Miss Kerr had an older son, who was also adopted.)

We finished lunch, and Miss Kerr said now that she had the phone number of my foster home, she would set up another time for us to hang out. I told her I couldn't wait.

But then . . . I never heard from her, which was really odd and disappointing. I was certain that Samuel wanted to stay connected with me. Like so many other things, it didn't make sense.

For all the turmoil in my life, something happened in the seventh grade that changed my world for the better.

One day in school, a teacher approached me in the hallway,

bent down on one knee, and said, "You must be Zion."

I typically don't like adults who bend down to speak to me because they think that's the only way I can understand them. In this case, the teacher bent down to show that he was my equal.

"I am," I said. He looked familiar—the chiseled physique, the crew cut, the jug ears, the piercing eyes. "You look just like Mr. Donahue," I said.

"He's my twin brother," Gil Donahue explained, "and I've heard about you." And he shook my hand firmly.

He taught history in the middle school and coached high school wrestling.

At the time, my foster parents were forcing me to wear prosthetics, which were made from carbon fiber and rubbed against my bones and soft tissue. They were supposed to help my spine, but they cut into my sides while also latching on to my feet, compounding the pain. I had been wearing them off and on for years and truly hated them. When I complained to my counselor in middle school, she called my foster parents; they got angry and made me wear the fake legs to bed.

I told Coach Donahue, the day I met him, what was going on.

"My legs are killing me," I said.

"So, you don't want to wear them anymore?"

"No, they're not me."

Coach Donahue went to the principal's office to discuss the matter, and from then on, whenever I went into his classroom, he said, "You can take your legs off." And some days I would keep them off and just walk around school normally, or at least what was normal for me.

Coach Donahue would also give me rides home on occasion. Once, when I wanted to enter a wrestling tournament, my foster parents wouldn't pay the fee, so Coach Donahue paid it and drove me to and from the event.

He was an important part of my life long before he became my coach. That he had known about me for years, from his twin brother, partly explains our connection. But I also think Coach Donahue saw in me a warrior spirit that, if given the chance, could one day flourish.

I was in eighth grade when my foster parents said they wanted to adopt me, and I was excited. I know that sounds bizarre, given all the hardships in the house, but it's something that every foster kid wants: a permanent home. I was tired of moving from house to house, and no matter how bad things were at my current place, they could be a lot worse at the next one. I also thought that once I was adopted, I would be treated better by these parents. I was close to one of the younger foster kids in the house—we had been together in three homes—and he was like my little brother. A court date was set for the adoption. Then I got into a fight with another foster kid in the house. I don't even recall what started it, and it doesn't matter.

You put a lot of kids together in the same space, and that's what happens.

The next morning, we were supposed to go to court to finalize the adoption. I had my shirt and tie laid out, and I had taken extra time to comb my hair. But when I went down for breakfast, the caseworker was already there—not to escort us to the courthouse but to remove me from the house. The parents, blaming me for the fight and for other alleged transgressions, were getting rid of me. What was supposed to be the happiest day of my life had turned into the worst.

The father just looked at me and said, "You're gone." I was packed and out before lunch.

I didn't want to leave because, as I said, even a bad home is better than an unknown one. Years later, when I had begun speaking publicly about my upbringing and its many challenges, I gave a talk at the Grace Hopper STEM Academy, in the Los Angeles area, a school for at-risk students who are ten to seventeen years old. Some of the students I spoke to had been trafficked, sexually assaulted, or abused in other ways. They had been thrown out of their homes and lived in the academy's foster dormitory. Nonetheless, many of those kids still wanted to return to their homes, regardless of the trauma.

"Very rarely do you find a kid who says, 'Home sucks. Find me another home,'" Bonita Bradshaw, one of the academy's founders, told me. "Kids are willing to go to back to dysfunctional situations because they know it as home."

I believe it.

Many foster kids have Lifebooks, which hold photos, drawings, and other mementos that document their journey through foster care. It's the kind of thing that kids really value when they're older as a reminder of all their experiences, good and bad, in foster care. I had a Lifebook, beginning with my days with Granny, but I left it at this one house that kicked me out. I later asked for it but never got it back.

My great fear—that the next house could be worse—turned out to be true.

My caseworker took me to a home in Alliance, about twenty-five miles northeast of Massillon, and I moved in with this nasty old Black woman who lived in the slums. My bedroom had plywood over the windows and smelled bad, and I didn't even have a blanket to sleep on. I heard gunshots at night, and when I cried out of fear, she told me to "shut the fuck up." She also said that she knew my biological mother and that I was a piece of shit just like her. The only television in the house was in her bedroom, which I wasn't allowed to watch. I instead had a DVD player with a screen, and whenever I stopped crying, she'd give me another Lord of the Rings movie.

I didn't have my own phone, so I felt more isolated than usual. I was tempted to run away. I was fourteen, it was the summer before I was to enter high school, and I was broken mentally. It was so bad that, using the landline, I called the family that had just kicked me out and begged to come back. They said no.

The caseworker showed up one day and said they had found another home back in Massillon. Did I want to go to it? I told her I didn't care where it was. Just get me out of there.

I was only in Alliance for two weeks, but the old lady got paid for a month.

CHAPTER 9
ON TOP OF THE WORLD

MASSILLON, Ohio, will never make anyone's list for Best Places to Live in America. It probably won't make anyone's list for Best Places to Live in Ohio, either, unless, of course, you're from Massillon. Then we'd be on it. The pride runs deep.

Never more than a speck on the map, Massillon was founded in 1853 on the banks of the Tuscarawas River. In the twentieth century, it was part of a roaring manufacturing region that produced the steel, iron, glass, and rubber that built America into a military and industrial power. Steel was Massillon's most important product; the city's factories made steel joists, engines, heat exchangers, roller bearings, castings, bottles, and indoor and outdoor signs. We even had a shovel company. The Massillon State Hospital for the Insane was a large, if offensively named, employer. (Today it is known as Heartland Behavioral Healthcare.)

Each group of European immigrants and their descendants—Greeks, Bulgarians, Albanians, Macedonians—had their own coffeehouse. Blacks had theirs as well. Jobs were plentiful, and Massillon attracted workers from across the region. These were the factory workers, born in Massillon or otherwise, who supported the grocers, diners, and retailers; who volunteered at civic organizations, charities, and booster clubs; and who filled the schools, sports venues, and churches.

The men (and some women as well) worked long hours in hot, noisy mills, and when their shifts were over, they headed out in their soot-covered overalls and grimy newsboy caps, often stopping at the corner saloon positioned strategically between the factory gates and residential areas.

Those days were long gone by the time I came around. Republic Steel was closed in 2002. (One worker scrawled on the wall, "Merry Christmas. You're fired.") But unlike other Ohio steel towns that saw declines in population (Canton, Youngstown, Steubenville, Warren), Massillon's population remained stable even after Big Steel fell on hard times: the city had about thirty-two thousand people in 1970, and it had that same number in 2020, as Massillon had diversified into light manufacturing and service businesses.

When I was growing up, the city was divided demographically. The East Siders were known as the "cake eaters"—lawyers and doctors. The West Siders were known as the steel mill guys. The kids on opposing sides weren't particularly fond of each other, and the rivalries played out in boxing rings, on ball fields, and in basketball gyms, sometimes organized by the Boys & Girls Club or the YMCA, sometimes by the kids themselves.

Even among young children, organized sports were

played fiercely. Massillon had a junior high school named Lorin Andrews, and it played its football games in "the old bottoms"—a field beneath one of the viaducts surrounded by wooded hills. After their opponent had arrived, the Lorin Andrews Dragons would walk across Lincoln Way and descend a steep hill through the woods. Still hidden, they would start clapping in rhythm, and as they got closer, the clapping got louder . . . and louder . . . and then the fans started clapping . . . and then the players burst through the tree line and screamed like hell as they raced onto the field. This was all designed to intimidate other seventh graders.

Massillon was always overshadowed by its larger neighbor, Canton, which has the landmark William McKinley memorial and the Pro Football Hall of Fame, two big tourist draws. Massillon has nothing so distinctive, but the locals say the town's pride and toughness have preserved it: three generations of working-class families didn't sling pig iron, haul masonry, and carry cement to see their city run over by Canton, and they sure as hell didn't survive rivers of liquid molten steel to see their city fade into oblivion.

What survived was that underdog, blue-collar spirit—and in my sport, wrestling, that meant when you won a match, it was like picking up your paycheck. Be happy but keep grinding. Life goes on. Your next opponent is also going to be tough. Your job is to be tougher.

I had no problem with that attitude. It was my nature.

. . .

I was fourteen when I moved back to Massillon from Alliance, but I was not on the East Side or the West Side. I was on Pearl Avenue on the Southeast Side, where most of the city's Black population lives. (Black residents make up about 10 percent of the population of Massillon.) The neighborhood wasn't as bad as the ghettos in Detroit or Cleveland or even Canton, but it was still the ghetto, at least as I saw it, and I was dead center in it.

I lived with Ella Kirkland, a gentle Black widow whose husband had built their one-story house, with a tiny kitchen, a basement, and a backyard swimming pool. She worked at a dry cleaner as a "spotter," removing stains from clothes. She was also a longtime foster mom who could take four boys at once. She typically had two boys when I lived there (though a fourth came and went), and we slept in one room in bunk beds. She ran a tight ship. She wouldn't let us walk through the front door because she didn't want anyone to dirty the living room. We entered through the kitchen door. She would wash our clothes, but we had to fold them and put them away. She said that if we left our dirty clothes under the bed, she would take them and keep them.

Mrs. Kirkland was a good foster mom, and I liked her. Her job at the dry cleaner ensured that my band uniform was always spotless. On Christmas Eve, she made a big dinner and invited over friends and family. Her most famous foster son was Shawn Crable, a football star in Massillon who played for the University of Michigan and was drafted by the New England Patriots. After an injury shortened his NFL career, Crable moved back to Massillon, and Mrs. Kirkland calls his three children her "grand-kiddies."

I liked Mrs. Kirkland for another reason: she told me I could stop taking Adderall and Vyvanse, which I had been on for four years. She assumed that I was overmedicated and that those drugs were bad news for me. I felt that as well, so I stopped cold turkey. It wasn't easy. I felt super-hyper for a full year, but the move off of them was long overdue. Some years later, I learned that Adderall and Vyvanse should not be taken together. Taken alone, each drug has a long list of side effects, including mood swings, high blood pressure, and irregular heartbeat, and each drug can be easily abused. Taking these drugs together, according to the Recovery Village Drug and Alcohol Rehab, which treats substance abuse, increases the risk of those side effects and the risk of abuse. I don't know which doctor wrote and renewed the prescriptions for me, but I do know that putting me on those two drugs simultaneously was a mistake.

For all of Mrs. Kirkland's good intentions, she couldn't do anything about the neighborhood.

One night, I woke up at two a.m. to get a drink of water. I looked through the window and saw a guy running through the street carrying a mini TV set and a Glock, chased by a couple of police cars. Other times I heard gunshots, just as I had in Alliance, and one night when we were sleeping, someone broke one of Mrs. Kirkland's windows. We lived two houses down from a home that had shoes hanging from a wire, which meant it was a drug house. I wasn't there long before some kids were shot and killed in a drug deal gone wrong. Shriver Park was just up the street, and thugs, gangbangers, and drug dealers hung out there. One night I was at the park with a girl, and on my way home in my wheelchair, a couple of dudes started following me. I sped down Glenwood Street, turned on Pearl, reached my house, and locked the door.

If dangers lurked outside of Mrs. Kirkland's home, tensions were often present inside as well. One challenge for any foster home is finding the right mix of kids, and in this case, the three of us were a volatile combination.

One kid was white and thought he was hard ghetto; the other kid was Black, and I had long despised him from school. I'll call him Jackson—tall, light skinned, nappy haired. He would hide my wheelchair. I'd throw his shoes in the pool. It was that kind of relationship.

Mrs. Kirkland didn't want the kids in her house hanging out on the street, and she thought she knew where we were at all times, but it wasn't hard to sneak out. After she went to bed, we'd just slip out the back door. While I had gotten into fights over the years and had not always applied myself in school, I had stayed out of serious trouble. That wouldn't last forever.

Though I moved around quite a bit, music was always prominent in my life, all the more so in high school.

Ever since I'd begun playing the trumpet, I had excelled through many hours of practice and had a good ear. I was usually the number-one trumpet player in whatever band I was in, and that was the case when I reached high school, where I was the number-one player for the Massillon High School marching band. This, however, is no ordinary marching band. It's called the Tiger Swing Band, and it's almost as famous as our football team.

In the 1930s, the team hired a musical director named George "Red" Bird, and he transformed the band from a military-style musical celebration into a contemporary theatrical performance. That meant colorful uniforms, popular music, complex dance routines, baton-twirling majorettes, and elaborate halftime shows. Other bands, from both high schools and colleges, emulated ours, so they became the norm across America. What you now see with any marching band, for any college or professional game—including the prime-time multimillion-dollar productions—originated in my little town of Massillon, Ohio.

Because I couldn't march, I played while either sitting off on the side or being pushed in my wheelchair. If you're the number-one trumpet player, it doesn't matter if you're disabled. I had to memorize three or four songs every week during the football season, and I played my heart out. Once, when we were performing at the Cuyahoga Falls band show, I was in my wheelchair, and during the routine, I was supposed to spin a girl around, who would then spin me—but when she did, the chair tipped over and I fell on my back. The crowd gasped. I just held my trumpet, closed my eyes, and never missed a beat.

That was how I learned to play in the first place: by closing my eyes and shutting out the rest of the world.

I was determined to do everything my peers did, no matter how many years it took. I wasn't allowed to go on roller coasters or Ferris wheels. I didn't care about Ferris wheels, but I certainly wanted to ride on roller coasters, the faster the better. When I was eight or nine, my family at the time drove all the way to Pittsburgh to spend the day at Kennywood, which had some great roller coasters. Even though the seats had tight straps, the amusement park wouldn't let me ride any of the coasters. The other kids went, and I waited at the bottom. It was always like that, and I hated amusement parks because I couldn't go on the best rides.

When I was a junior in high school, the swing band went to Universal Studios in Orlando, Florida, and performed some Disney songs. We then got to enjoy the park. One of the park's best rides is the Hollywood Rip Ride Rockit, whose top speed is sixty-five miles per hour and whose passengers must be at least four foot three to ride. I was more than one foot too short, but I really wanted to ride it, and I was tired of being denied.

I had to go on it.

My friends thought I was crazy, but we got in line and avoided eye contact with any attendant, and, being as inconspicuous as a Black teenager without legs can be, I stepped onto a moving sidewalk that traveled at the same pace as the coaster. Each chair holds two passengers. I hopped into the chair, so did one of my friends, and the attendant put down my thick yellow plastic waist belt with a metal bar without saying anything and moved to the next person. I was in!

The coaster lurched ahead on the red track, and we inched up and up and up and then . . . we bolted straight down in one exhilarating plunge, and we were twisting and turning and screaming, and then ascending skyward, aloft more than 150 feet, and once again hurtling to the earth and then careening out of a turn. I gripped that crossbar as if my life depended on it, because my life did depend on it. It was the most thrilling one minute and thirty-nine seconds of my life.

I loved the breakneck, delirious speed of the coaster. But even more, I loved how it felt to defy one of the many rules that had always constricted me from just being a kid.

CHAPTER 10
CHAMPIONS ARE MADE WHEN NO ONE IS WATCHING

ALTHOUGH I DID long to be like other kids, that wasn't enough for me. I wanted to excel, and I knew what I wanted to excel in: wrestling. I wrestled year after year, all through elementary school and middle school, but all I did was lose. I'm sure some of my opponents felt sorry for me, but they still beat me. I was basically a sideshow who got sympathetic applause from other parents but no glory, no medals, no satisfaction. Then I reached high school, where the competition was much tougher and where someone with my disability seemingly had no chance. But I refused to quit. I kept wrestling and was on the junior varsity during my sophomore and junior seasons. Nothing changed, however. I continued to lose. I was still a sideshow.

But the Massillon wrestling team was different. I had someone there who was invested in me, supported me, and wouldn't let me fail.

Gil Donahue had helped me when I was in junior high and tracked me as a student and wrestler ever since. He heard teachers complain that I was rebellious, didn't do my homework, wasn't a good kid. He didn't believe that last part. He knew my home life was a mess. He didn't know the details but assumed that it was dragging me down. Through the wrestling boosters club, Coach Donahue gave me gift cards to Subway to make sure I had enough to eat. I wasn't the only one. Massillon had other kids who were near or below the poverty line. One wrestler was sleeping in a car.

Coach Donahue also heard the other kids taunt me, particularly in junior high. Sometimes behind my back, sometimes to my face. He thought I was more intent on lashing out than in developing my own identity: I was this angry Black kid with no legs and no family and no home. I was defined by what I didn't have, but what *did* I have? And who was I really?

I didn't know myself—I was just trying to survive—but Coach Donahue wanted to help me find out. He also liked the idea of taking kids off the scrap heap and turning them into something. He knew a lot of those guys.

Gil Donahue had grown up in South Canton; he was a wiry, smart-aleck child whose best friend and chief rival was his twin brother, Greg, who would become my art teacher at Orchard Hill Intermediate School. Their father was a disciplinarian who worked at a Ford plant for forty-four years, often on twelve-hour shifts. Gil spent his days in the gym at the YMCA and discovered wrestling there at age ten. He fell in love with it. The sport wasn't that popular in the 1970s—it was only seasonal and had little prestige in football-mad Ohio. But even at a young age, Gil liked the one-on-one battles and the whole idea of imposing your will on another human being.

He wasn't big, however, and wasn't a great athlete. But he was competitive, and he came to realize that he could win by out-lifting, out-working, and out-hustling his opponents, even if that required many hours by himself.

"The people who want to be the best," he tells me, "are the ones who are the loneliest."

He wasn't entirely lonely, as Greg also wrestled, and their matches against each other were epic. They wrestled in high school, but they didn't want to compete against each other when the stakes were so high. Wrestling is segmented by weight class, so this allowed the brothers to avoid each other on the mat: sometimes one brother would cut weight and go down a class (perhaps to 120 pounds), and sometimes the other brother would cut weight. Gil was a three-time district qualifier but never made the state tournament. Still, that was good enough to wrestle at Ashland University. The school gave Gil half a scholarship and Greg the other half so that their father only had to pay one tuition, and the twins continued their ritual of reducing or adding weight so that they never had to compete against each other.

The jump from high school athletics to college is huge, and Gil was hardly the most talented, but he reached nationals two consecutive years and traveled to Russia and wrestled against its Olympic team. His work ethic was his edge.

"You have to do things," he tells me, "that other people don't want to do at times they don't want to do it."

After college, he got a job as a substitute teacher at GlenOak High School in North Canton and was also an assistant wrestling coach. When GlenOak had a match against Massillon in 1996, Gil's passion for the sport caught the eye of Massillon wrestling coach Mike Skelly. A native of Massillon, Coach Skelly was in the midst of a lengthy career that would see him coach sixty-seven different teams across many sports, boys and girls, high school and junior high. He was demanding and rugged, but he never cussed and wouldn't let the players cuss, either.

After the season ended, Coach Skelly called Gil and offered him a job as Massillon's assistant wrestling coach. Gil accepted, and two years later, when Coach Skelly stepped down, he became the head coach. He was only twenty-six but knew what it would take to build a championship program. On his first day on the job, he posted a big sign in the locker room: **CHAMPIONS ARE MADE WHEN NO ONE IS WATCHING.**

Even when I wasn't that good, I loved wrestling for the same reason that the ancient Greeks loved it; they introduced it into the Olympics as the first contest of strength. I also love wrestling for the same reason that the writers of the Old

Testament included it in the Bible or that a poet from ancient Mesopotamia invoked it in the *Epic of Gilgamesh*. Wrestling does more than separate winners and losers; it defines the character of the combatants as few other sports do.

Its appeal is its primal, solitary nature: it rewards strength, endurance, and will, and it demands accountability. There are no teammates who can share the credit or the blame—you're not a running back who needs a block or a power forward who needs an outlet pass. You're just one guy, and you're on the mat against a single opponent.

If you've spent your life watching other sports on television, you won't understand the pace and rhythm of wrestling. There are no time-outs and no breaks to talk to coaches, to take a breath, to change plans, to regroup. A high school wrestling match is three two-minute periods, plus, if needed, overtime called "blood rounds." A match may seem short, but it's actually a marathon. No other sport demands constant physical contact in the same way wrestling does. Each bout is a body-twisting, high-impact, intricate chess match—move, countermove, move, countermove, "taking shots" for takedowns, escapes, and pins.

The clock keeps running, and no matter what the score, you always have a chance to win. That possibility also separates wrestling from most other sports. If you're losing by a huge margin in basketball, football, hockey, or soccer, and only a few seconds remain, you have no chance of winning.

If you're losing by a huge margin in wrestling and only a few seconds remain, you can still pin your opponent before the match ends and win. That's why **NEVER GIVE UP** is such an important mantra among wrestlers. Until that final whistle sounds, you always have a chance.

Football players who try to wrestle typically lose weight because they've never had to work so hard. Wrestling doesn't have the violent collisions of football, but a wrestler's body is torqued, threshed, and slammed in ways that never happen on the football field. In wear and tear, one year of wrestling is like five years of football.

Just making a high school varsity wrestling team is uniquely competitive and unforgiving. Only one wrestler competes in each weight class, and to be that alpha male competitor, you must beat everyone at your weight. In other words, the wrestlers themselves decide who makes the team, not the coaches. Even after the season begins, an underling can challenge the top dog, and if the underling wins, he takes the spot. Coaches encourage those challenges throughout the season to create a hyper-competitive environment in which doggedness is rewarded and complacency is punished.

Boxing shares the one-on-one intensity of wrestling, but a boxing match can be decided by one lucky punch that knocks out an opponent. Luck is rarely a factor in wrestling, nor are there bad bounces or Hail Mary passes or any other unexpected turns that can decide a match. Wrestling referees will make disputed calls, but for the most part, the sport is too confined, the elements too controlled, for randomness to determine outcomes.

This is what makes wrestling the greatest sport. The better wrestler *on that day* is going to triumph. Me against you.

And when the referee raises your arm, you don't leap in the air or showboat. That's for the glamour sports. You shake hands with your opponent and his coaches, you recognize the shared sacrifice, and you celebrate with humility.

It took me a long time to get to the winner's circle, but Coach Donahue had a plan—for me and the entire program.

CHAPTER 11
THE CASTAWAY KIDS

MASSILLON had never had a strong wrestling program, but Coach Donahue figured this was a steel town, lots of tough kids. He just had to convince the community, and some of those kids, about the virtues of wrestling. In doing so, he ran into the most powerful force in Massillon: high school football. The sport is hallowed throughout Ohio, only more so in my hometown.

Part of it is history: Massillon's first game was in 1894. That year, Massillon played McKinley High School, in Canton, a rivalry that exists to this day. The matchup has become prominent nationally to the point that Vegas takes bets on it and, according to the coach Mike Skelly, ESPN places Massillon versus McKinley right next to Ohio State versus University of Michigan as the best football rivalries in America. When a Massillon-McKinley game was canceled in the 1960s due to a flu outbreak, they played twice the following year. These games can attract more than twenty thousand fans.

The city of Massillon also fielded one of the first professional football teams in the early 1900s, and our city's most famous resident is the late Paul Brown, who played on the high school team and coached it for nine years (his record was 80–8–2). He coached Cleveland's first NFL team from 1946 to 1962 (hence their name, the Cleveland Browns). He then began an NFL team in Cincinnati and wanted to pay homage to his beloved Massillon Tigers: he chose the same colors, orange and black, but named them the Bengals instead of the Tigers. Only one team in Ohio could be called the Tigers.

Paul Brown is buried in Massillon, and before each high school game at Paul Brown Stadium, located next to the high school on 1 Paul E Brown Drive, the players congregate around the Paul Brown statue and say a prayer.

Football teams are royalty in many small towns, but Massillon takes its exaltation to the extreme. For decades, orange footballs were placed in hospital bassinets of newborn boys. There are men who insist on being buried in their orange Tiger sweatshirt and cap. Caskets with the image of Obie, the tiger mascot, are popular. Tiger balloons, tiger-striped cars, and tiger underwear are all part of the scene.

A football boosters club, combined with local donors, ensures that everything is first class. The football team currently has a massive indoor facility and three full-size fields. One year, before a playoff game, a helicopter flew in new helmets.

At least thirty Massillon graduates have played professional football, none more prominent than Chris Spielman, who played for Massillon in the 1980s. He was a star linebacker at Ohio State and played in the NFL. When he was in high school, Spielman was entered in a Wheaties contest sponsored by General Mills, which determined the winner in part by how much cereal the community ate. Massillon rallied around the kitchen table. Spielman won, and afterward the company came to his house and said, "There's no way in the world one community can eat that much Wheaties."

We support our football players.

Coach Donahue could never make wrestling an equal to football, but he needed to make it alluring enough so that more athletes, particularly football players, would join. He created recruiting posters in which the wrestlers posed in a football stance, implying, correctly, that wrestling will improve your football skills. He went around to different businesses in Massillon, from coffee shops to copier stores, and posted the season schedule on their walls. He visited the local newspaper and encouraged it to cover the team. He persuaded the school's television production team to broadcast matches on the school channel. He organized the building of a big wrestling float for the Massillon-McKinley football parade.

But it was still a struggle. While the football team was awash in money, the wrestlers had years in which the school paid only for tournament fees and buses, while the boosters club had to raise money for uniforms. It didn't help that the head football coach was also always the athletic director, ensuring that football always received disproportionate funds (and guaranteeing that the football coach received a far higher salary than all other coaches).

The head football coach, for sure, is under enormous pressure. If he loses more games than he wins, he won't last long. The football coach also expects undivided loyalty from his players, and I know that from personal experience. My senior year, I decided to play football, which has been done by other kids who either didn't have their full legs or who only had one leg. I knew I could do it, and I thought it would make me a better wrestler.

At practice, I was good at tackling. I'm already low to the ground, and I'm just as fast, in short distances, as most people on two legs. I loved the violence of football, and during drills, I would cut down running backs at the ankles. I played defensive tackle and could slip past blockers to get to the quarterback. I was second string and was looking forward to the season, but after practice one day, I asked the coach if I could go to a wrestling practice as well while the two seasons overlapped. He said no, so I hung up my jersey and my helmet and never went back.

The football coaches didn't even want their guys to play other sports after their season ended. They wanted them to lift weights during the winter and deterred the players from joining other teams. Coach Donahue lamented that these coaches thought they had a monopoly on the players. In his twenty years at Massillon, he dealt with five different football coaches, always fighting the same battle.

But the struggle was fitting. Wrestlers are never the stars in high schools, colleges, or the pros, and certainly not in Massillon. A lot of us really didn't have places to go; as the assistant wrestling coach Percy McGhee Jr. put it, we were "the castaway kids."

Black wrestlers, meanwhile, are rare. Some of the best wrestlers ever are Black—Lee Kemp, Jordan Burroughs, Joey Davis—but there aren't many of us. Wrestling has little presence in Black pop culture and doesn't represent any kind of gateway to success for Black youth.

None of that mattered to me because I never really fit in anywhere regardless. I was at home with the castaways.

Wrestling matches are often determined after the first person wears out, so Coach Donahue had a clear approach on how to prepare us. First, get us exhausted. That meant lots of cardio. Wind sprints. Intense drills. Get us to the point where we want to quit. Then teach us. When we're on the mat and beaten down and close to tears, that's when we really focus. As Coach Donahue saw it, the practices had to be more grueling than the matches, or, as he liked to say, "The dress rehearsal should be far worse than the performance."

He also wanted to prepare us mentally. "What is your mindset?" he'd ask us. "What are you thinking about when you're on the mat? I want you thinking about all the stuff you've been through. Has your opponent been through that? No. Has your opponent made the sacrifices you've made? No. So you're going to win."

"Losing," he'd say, "is not a sometime thing, it's an all-time thing. You don't win some of the time. You win all of the time."

He wanted us to take pride in the letters across our chest. "Massillon was here long before we were, and it will be here long after we're gone. It's way bigger than us. So we have to wrestle for us, and the 'us' is the *M* on our chest."

He was adamant that he wasn't just teaching us how to win in wrestling.

"You wrestle with things your entire life," he'd tell us. "You wrestle with your relationships—with God, with your wife, with your children. There will be a lot to overcome, and you have to know how to push through and not give up on yourself."

He believed that wrestling was the perfect metaphor for life. Wrestling rewards individual achievement, yet no wrestler can win a meet or a tournament by himself. This isn't a sport in which one dominant player can win a game by scoring thirty points, pitching a no-hitter, or catching a touchdown pass. One dominant wrestler can only win one match in a dual meet or tournament. If his teammates don't win in their weight classes, his team loses.

As Coach Donahue saw it, wrestling was indeed a lonely road, but it was also about young men embracing the same sacrifice, a team endeavor in which each player's destiny is intertwined with that of the others. We were, in his words, a wolf pack.

"After your match," he'd say, "come back to the wolf pack, lick your wounds, make your adjustments, and then go back out and fight for that wolf pack."

Coach Donahue eventually established Massillon as a force in wrestling, sending two or three wrestlers to state each year and placing one or two of them. His first state champion, Ivan McClay, won in 2013. And when the football team had an off year, he'd tell his squad, "We have to hold the banner for Massillon!"

And we did.

In 2012, I joined the wolf pack as a freshman, but I was also a breed apart.

CHAPTER 12
THE STREET LIFE

WHILE WRESTLING AND MUSIC gave me structure, I had a very different life beyond the walls of high school, and my teachers and coaches knew very little about it. In the summer of 2012, just a month shy of my fifteenth birthday and right before I entered Massillon High School, I got into the most serious trouble of my life. I had just moved into Mrs. Kirkland's house, and I have no one to blame but myself.

It was a warm, lazy day, and I was sitting outside Mrs. Kirkland's house. A skinny Black kid decided to walk across the yard. Mrs. Kirkland was particular about such things. She didn't like people walking on her front lawn. She asked this kid not to walk on her grass, but he mouthed off at her. He disrespected her. I didn't like that, and this was one more time that I let my anger get the better of me.

"If you want to talk like that," I told him, "go somewhere else. But if you want to take this to another level, I'm good with that also."

He stayed on the property.

"Bro," I said. "You gotta get outta here."

He stayed.

So we fought for about ten minutes. I'm sure he thought I'd be easy to whip, but I kicked his ass, and I showed him no mercy. I broke his collarbone and jaw and snapped his wrist. It was brutal, but I felt he deserved it.

Two days later, the cops showed up, arrested me for assault, and put me in handcuffs. They put me in their police car, but with my hands behind my back, I could barely sit up. When we got to the station, they had to carry me in because I couldn't walk. They took my snapback hat and my watch, fingerprinted me, and took my picture. I was charged and made to wait in a holding room.

Mrs. Kirkland got me out, and then I went to court. Had I been sixteen, I would have been tried as an adult, but because but because I wasn't fifteen yet, the penalties were less severe. I had a hearing before a judge. I didn't show it, but I was nervous. I had heard the stories about prison. I didn't think someone like me would do well in there.

The judge was a middle-aged white woman who had a kind face and seemed willing to listen. I told her exactly what I had done and why—this kid disrespected Mrs. Kirkland, and I told him to leave the property. When he didn't, I made him pay.

The judge nodded but told me I could not go around

beating up other people. She gave me the option of three months at the Indian River Juvenile Correctional Facility in Massillon or two years on probation. I didn't want to go to any correctional facility, particularly not Indian River. It was near a wastewater treatment plant on the south side of town, and it didn't smell so great over there. So I chose probation, and for the next two years, I had a probation officer and caseworker come to the house every month to see if I was staying out of trouble.

It was better than Indian River, but every time I had to leave the state for a wrestling match, I had to go to court and get permission. I hated that.

Even the most basic things in my life became sources of resentment. My school bus was one of them. I wanted to take the regular school bus, but as ordered by the state, I had to take a so-called handicap bus, provided by the city, for students with special needs. In my case, that bus was also used to take me to my high school wrestling matches and band events. The bus had an electronic lift for anyone in a wheelchair, and it had space in the back where the wheelchairs, with the kids in them, could be secured to the floor. Otherwise, it was a normal bus. When the band traveled, we had four regular buses and one handicap bus, though everyone was able-bodied except me.

I didn't like riding that bus. On rides to and from school, it carried students with a range of disabilities: Down syndrome, multiple sclerosis, various mental and behavior challenges. It also provided door-to-door service. But I didn't like the bus because I didn't see myself as disabled, and—though I can't prove this—I thought they put some disruptive kids on that bus just to punish them, as if misbehavior was itself a disability.

I gladly defied the handicap bus. The bus monitor, Debbie McGuire, had known me for many years (she was the woman who cleaned me up after my adoptive mother hit me with a chair). Once I was on the bus, Mrs. McGuire would strap my wheelchair down in the back, but instead of sitting in it, I would just hop off and sit in a regular seat. I typically used the electronic lift, because that's what I was instructed to do, but one time when I was living with Mrs. Kirkland, one of the boys in the house hid my wheelchair, so I had to go to school without it. When the bus came, I just climbed up the steps using my arms and took my seat.

By my sophomore year, I took that bus a lot less, and I either pushed myself to school or found a ride.

One good thing about the handicap bus was Mrs. McGuire. She was on that bus not only during my trips to and from elementary school, middle school, and high school, but she was also required to travel with me to my wrestling matches and band events. We got to know each other very well.

She was an institution, as she rode the handicap bus for twenty-seven years, only retiring after COVID-19 made it too dangerous for her. She wanted to ride that bus to help the kids who needed help, making her a lot like the Schmuckers. She lived in Massillon, and I had a lot of respect for her family because one of her kids, Travis, was a high school football star. Mrs. McGuire can tell you off the top of her head Travis's stats his senior year in 1991: how many carries he had (205), how many yards he gained (1,979), how many touchdowns he had against McKinley (5). She also worked at the home football games, doing a job that nobody wanted, controlling the student section. And she could get everyone's attention just by lifting or lowering her arm. No one could control the stadium like she could.

Mrs. McGuire looked out for me. When our band traveled to a football game or to a competition, I often didn't have money for food. But one of her grandsons, Tayveon, would hang out with me, and Mrs. McGuire would give him a few extra dollars so I could get something to eat.

She would often compliment me and say how well I was doing. She would also ask me how I was feeling. I would tell her the good stuff but never the bad stuff—I disclosed the bad stuff to very few adults. But Mrs. McGuire saw me so often over the years, she could usually tell when I was upset and would encourage me to keep my head up.

Because of the chaos in my homes, I was sometimes late for the bus, and she would remind me that riding this bus was a privilege and that I had to appreciate what other people were doing for me. One time I was seven or eight minutes late, and she was clearly frustrated.

"You have to understand," she said, "you are blessed that we have a bus that buses you to school, but we're also doing you a favor."

I made some excuse about her not knowing what my life was like (though in retrospect, I would guess that she probably did).

She looked at me and said, "God has His hands on you, and you can accomplish anything you want."

For all the bad things that happened in my youth, I always had adults who tried to keep me on the right path and who thought I could make it. But once I got to high school, even someone like Mrs. McGuire couldn't steer me away from trouble.

Being on probation didn't straighten me out. It just made me more bitter. I didn't get along with the other kids in Mrs. Kirkland's house, didn't have many friends, wasn't doing well in school, and just didn't feel connected or grounded. While

I was good at music and art and loved to wrestle, I had no dreams beyond survival, no expectations of a better life. I needed something different, and I found it on the streets of Massillon.

I started running with a couple guys in the neighborhood who were connected to gangs. I don't think my motivations were that different from those of most kids. If a kid sees someone ride a bike, he's going to want to ride a bike. If that same kid sees someone walk into a store and steal a candy bar, he's going to want to do the same thing if there isn't something better for him at home. If that kid's home life is empty, the street life is going to look appealing.

It did for me, and if I was an unusual sight on a wrestling mat, I was surely the same on the streets of Massillon. But I think the street guys respected me because they knew I had been through a lot. That I didn't back down from anybody gave me more cred than most would-be gangsters.

Some of these guys were in their twenties and thirties and had been in and out of prison. They didn't use their real names in case someone snitched, though that probably wasn't going to happen. If you did that, they'd kill you. One guy always kept a gun on his hip. Another guy's home had a shotgun on the coffee table, an AK-47 hanging from one wall, and a Ruger in the nightstand.

At fourteen, I was now smoking blunts and trapping—

selling drugs. If someone's house was hot (being watched by the cops), I would take a brick of coke and hide it under my bunk until that house was clear. We'd do dumb stuff, like pulling up to a supermarket in the dead of night and smashing the carts in back. Or more serious stuff, like stealing from Walmart. We'd break into the Apple case and use wire cutters to free the iPod Touches, and we'd hide them under the seat of my wheelchair. When we'd walk out the doors, the alarm would sound, and the security guard would pat everyone down.

Then he'd ask me, "Is there anything on you?"

I'd say, "No, sir. I'm just in my wheelchair."

I'd even hop off and let him pat me down and inspect the chair. He'd never find the iPods, and off we went.

Other times, I'd be walking through a store on my hands and would hide stuff in my jacket. I'm so low to the ground, no one thought to look at me or believed I was suspicious.

An iPod Touch cost about three hundred dollars, but we knew how to upsell and would tell buyers, "Hey, man. This is the newest one. We'll let you have it for only a grand. You got to have it." And we'd sell it for a thousand bucks. There were ten of us, so we'd each clear a hundred dollars. Sometimes, we'd find easy marks and sell each phone for two thousand dollars. We exploited stupid people. That was the business model.

I helped find some of these marks myself, at Massillon High School. Massillon is not a rich city, but we do have our affluent white families, and I knew how to hustle.

"Hey, man," I'd say. "Do you know anybody who wants this iPod Touch? I got a good deal. Two grand for the newest one. You can get it out here. Just hit me up. You know where I live. Just pull up to my spot, and we'll go to my boy's house and get it."

The kid would pull up—or maybe his older brother, cousin, or friend—and we'd make the deal. Sometimes we'd trick him: I would stand back, and the bangers would rough the guy up, take his money, and keep the iPod, which we would then sell to someone else. Four grand, just like that.

Sometimes we broke into the high school, as I was strong enough to rip one of the door handles off. We'd typically smoke some weed and hang out, though one time a guy said, "I'm going to break into the vending machine."

"How you going to do that?"

"Just watch."

He took out some tools, opened the machine, and a gush of silver loot came pouring out. We walked away with it.

The high school itself is located near the ghetto, which we called Mill-Q, because an old mill was nearby, and we put a *Q* on the end: it was just our signature. When white kids walked through, we'd look at them from our porches and say, "What are you doing in Mill-Q, nigga? Better get out of here before someone robs you."

This was my life for more than two years, and I had plenty of close calls. There were two bad parts of town—the one I lived in, which was just east of the Tuscarawas River, and the other just west of the river on Tremont Avenue. A nonprofit used a church there to help kids who needed a haven or food, and I would go over on Mondays. One time, a couple of friends told me they were going to buy some weed, and they asked me if I wanted to join them. I said sure. We walked to an empty lot down the street to make the buy, but the seller thought we hadn't given him enough money. He pulled a Glock out of his shorts and pointed it right at my face. I was petrified but couldn't show any fear or weakness. In that moment, staying cool was my best chance. I stood within inches of that gun barrel for what seemed like an eternity, and my main thought was, *Dog, if you're going to do it, do it* and *Let's get it over with.*

My friends didn't have any more money. All I had was two dollars. I pulled the bills from my pocket and gave them to him. He walked away.

I learned a lot on the street: they don't call it "street smarts" for nothing. I learned who to avoid, how to look at people, how to win over someone's trust or loyalty. I also knew that gang life was reckless, but I didn't care. These guys were a family, the closest thing to family I'd ever had, a family that didn't abuse or neglect me. We hung out together, we stole together, we protected each other. When I thought about the future, I wanted to be a thug. I knew I'd probably end up in jail or dead, but that's what I knew, and I was good with that.

Meanwhile, my time with Mrs. Kirkland soon came to an end.

Tensions always ran high between Jackson and me. We had to sleep in the same bedroom, use the same bathroom, eat at the same table. We had no separation. One time we got into a fight, and he had me on the ground and cut me with a knife. I told him, "If you let me up, I will kill you."

Mrs. Kirkland found us and ended the fight before anyone was more seriously injured.

On Thanksgiving of my junior year, there would be no such intervention.

It was morning, and Mrs. Kirkland's family, including her biological son and her previous foster children, were starting to come over. I had to take a shower in the basement bathroom, but Jackson lay on the floor and wouldn't let me get by. We argued, and when I tried to step over him, he knocked me over, and we started brawling again. He initially had me in a choke hold, but I got loose and put his face into the wall. I then went upstairs, hoping this would be the end of it.

It wasn't.

Later that day, when I was in the basement hanging out,

Jackson brought over a friend, and they came down together to settle the score. The basement had a wet bar, and I jumped on the counter, grabbed a metal chair, and told them, "If you back up, I'll put this chair down. But if you come toward me, I'll crack this on your head. I'm not playing, bro."

They came toward me. I lifted the chair and swung it over my head, but it got stuck in the ceiling, and I had to let it go. I next grabbed an empty bottle of Jack Daniels and smashed it against the back of the neck of Jackson's friend.

Mrs. Kirkland heard the ruckus, came downstairs, and ended the fight. It was also the end for me at her house.

"I'm going to have to remove you," she said.

I looked her in the eye and said, "Do it. I don't care."

I was nothing if not honest, because I didn't care. I was seventeen, which meant I was one year away from aging out of the foster care system. And the system had a name for that: "emancipation."

Yes, emancipation, which is the word for liberation from bondage or, I guess, from the foster care system.

As a practical matter, it would mean that the state of Ohio would no longer have direct responsibility over me. I'd be an orphan in every sense of the word—from family and from state. Mrs. Kirkland and my caseworker decided that I'd stay at her house in Massillon until the semester ended, and then I would be sent to a group home in Cincinnati. I knew group homes had a terrible reputation as dumping grounds for kids who got kicked out of foster homes, that they were less like homes and more like places of incarceration. What's more, I had never been to Cincinnati, and I didn't know anyone in Cincinnati. But that's where I would be.

And once I hit eighteen, I'd be on the streets, emancipated.

CHAPTER 13
YOU'VE TRIED EVERYTHING ELSE; TRY GOD

IN 2011, two children's advocacy organizations—First Star and Children's Advocacy Institute—published "The Fleecing of Foster Children: How We Confiscate Their Assets and Undermine Their Financial Security." It noted that American parents gave on average almost fifty thousand dollars in assistance to their children after age eighteen to help them achieve self-sufficiency, and they also often provided nonfinancial support: a home to live in, career guidance, unconditional love.

Foster children who age out of the system at eighteen receive none of that, at least not from the system that raised them. About thirty thousand of the nation's foster children age out of the system each year, and according to the report, only 2 percent to 3 percent earn a higher-education degree. By age twenty-four, fewer than half are employed, and they earn less than half, on average, than their peers with no history of foster care. Also by that age, 37 percent have experienced homelessness or had "couch surfed," and up to 85 percent of all foster youth experience mental health issues.

All these problems are intertwined and, according to the report, because foster care alumni don't have a family safety net, "a negative outcome in any one of these areas can spiral into a lifetime of poverty."

Those were my prospects as I entered the Christmas season of my junior year at Massillon High School, although I thought mine were worse. Had I been emancipated, I'm certain that within a few years, I would have been on the streets, locked up, or dead.

I was living with Mrs. Kirkland until the semester ended. I was still in the band, and we had a holiday performance at the school. Unknown to me, Kimberlli Hawkins was in the audience. She was a foster mom in Massillon, a thickset, light-skinned Black woman with long ringletted hair. Her daughter Indy was a year ahead of me in school. My caseworker had told Miss Kim about me, but she didn't know I played in the band.

I guess I was easy to spot.

Miss Kim saw me walk across the stage with my trumpet and hop onto the platform. She later told me that she saw something special in me that night. Even though she knew about my checkered past, she did not let that define her view of me. Whatever she saw in me, I believe, was due to her faith in God and a personal story that was almost as harrowing as mine.

Or as she later told me, "I got a bad start but a strong finish."

Miss Kim's maiden name is Clark, and she was born in 1970 and grew up in Canton with two younger brothers, Darnell and Okey. Talk about a family with sports in its blood. Darnell was a football standout at McKinley High School who played running back for Youngstown State, led the team to two national championships, and was elected to the school's hall of fame. Okey was also a high school football star; he played at Mount Union College (now University of Mount Union) in Alliance. Their younger cousin Carlin Isles attended Jackson High School in Massillon, was an all-county football player, a two-time state champion in track, and later joined the United States national rugby team. Called the "fastest man in American rugby," he played on the American Olympic team in 2016 and 2020.

Kim was also a runner and could have gone to college on a track scholarship, but her life took a different turn.

When she was in high school in the late 1980s, her parents separated, and she lived with her mother in public housing. Her mother worked full-time and also went to school, eventually earning a master's degree; she sacrificed everything, according to Kim, and raised her children right. But Kim was often left unsupervised, and at McKinley High School, she started running with the gangs, fighting, smoking weed, and drinking. She was kicked out of McKinley, so she transferred to Timken Senior High School in Canton, but she failed to graduate.

She got married at eighteen—her husband was in the military—and their daughter, Quamarri, who goes by Quay, was born two years later. They were stationed at Fort Eustis, in Virginia, but the couple separated two years later, and in 1992, Kim and Quay moved back to Ohio. But Kim didn't believe she could take care of her child and gave up custody. "I had to put my pride on the table," she tells me. "I didn't even go to court to fight for her."

Instead, Quay moved in with her paternal grandmother in Alliance while Kim returned to Canton and saw her daughter only on weekends. She now knows how odd it looks—the woman who would take in abandoned children, me included, chose not to maintain custody of her first child. But at the time, she knew she was making the right decision. "When you're lying in bed at night, you can't run from yourself," she says, "and I knew Quay would be better with her grandma."

Kim returned to the life that she knew best—life on the streets.

She sold drugs. She ran with gangs. She got into fights. She had her apartment raided twice by the police in search of drugs. She was detained in custody.

"It didn't make me smarter," she says. "It just made me better at being bad."

The years passed, and Kim eventually lost her apartment and moved in with her mother. But Kim remained angry, and her mother wouldn't tolerate her behavior. One day when Kim came home, her stuff was piled into two large plastic trash bags and left outside. This was 1996, and at age twenty-six, she was now homeless.

Kim showed up at other people's doors, looking for a couch to sleep on and willing to exchange sex for a place to stay. She got pregnant and had another girl, Indonesia, who goes by Indy. Kim was now homeless, jobless, and a single mom.

She found a place to stay with a cousin in a Canton housing project, Chip Townhouses, which is known as the Chips. She had various hustles for money, and when her cousin moved out, she let Kim and Indy stay in the apartment. And it was there one night, in that crummy public housing project, sitting at a table with a blunt and a Double Deuce beer, that Kim hit rock bottom. She looked at Indy on the couch, and she thought she heard the devil speak: "Just kill her and you," he said, "and she will be at peace."

Kim was raised to both love God and fear God—she often watched her mother pray, and each Sunday a bus took her and her brothers to church. When she now heard the devil tell her to take her own life and that of her child, she didn't know if she would end up in hell: it was possible that death was even worse than life.

Then she heard her mother's voice, words that she had often heard when she was growing up: "You've tried everything else; try God."

Until that moment, God was—in Kim's words—just a "story," but now she blurted out, crying and cussing: "Lord, if you're real, I need you to manifest yourself, because I've messed up so bad, and I ain't got nothing!"

That's when the Holy Spirit met her—that night, in the

kitchen—and said to her, "I will bring you out of the muck and mire."

She listened and she felt the words in her heart, and from that moment on, He has been with her.

She started going to church, listening to sermons, reading the Bible. At some point, she heard a phrase that stuck with her: "God wouldn't take you through troubled waters if He knew you couldn't swim." She could swim; she was sure of that. But her mind and her soul had to be renewed, she had to trust God, and then with God's blessings, she would try to swim free.

She began eliminating friends who were no good for her. She went back to school and earned her GED. She found a job as an EMT. She and Indy landed their own place in Mahoning Manor public housing. When a friend wanted to use it to sell drugs, Kim said no, and that friendship ended.

In 2002, Kim saw a job opening at the Stark Metropolitan Housing Authority, and she figured this job, in security, was a good fit. She'd been living in its apartments for years. She got to the office on Tuscarawas Street in Canton just before the 4:30 p.m. deadline for applications. She had the interview, but several days passed. The weekend came and, assuming she had not gotten the job, she wanted to smoke a blunt but couldn't find one. Then on Monday, the housing authority called her and said she had the job—but she had to pass a drug test. Had she smoked the blunt, she would have failed the test and been rejected, but she passed and was hired.

It wasn't luck or fate, Kim thought. It was evidence of God's handiwork.

"If the Lord had closed that door, I wouldn't be in this place now," she says. "God always has a plan."

She has worked at the housing authority ever since and is now the receptionist, or as some would call it, "the director of first impressions."

"That's the hard part about faith," she says. "We want to see it. We want to know it's tangible. But that's not how faith works. He says, 'You trust me first, and then I'll show you.'"

The year Kim began at the housing authority, she and Indy moved out of the projects in Canton and into a so-called scattered site in Massillon, subsidized, low-income housing on Fairlawn Avenue near Perry High School. (The street is in Perry Township but is considered part of Massillon.) It was a significant improvement, and the move coincided with Indy entering first grade. She was now a latchkey kid. Each day at work, Kim would call home, but she didn't want Indy picking up the phone unless it was Kim on the other end. So Kim would let the phone ring once and hang up, then repeat, and then on the third call, Indy knew it was her mom and picked up. When cell phones came along, Kim always kept a landline in her house—she had to know that Indy was in the house physically and not wandering the streets.

She was also strict, determined to prevent Indy from making the same mistakes she had made. She spanked or grounded Indy when she got out of line, took her to church and Bible study, and drove her to her sporting events. She had always been part of Quay's life, and in 2017, Quay moved into public housing around the corner from her mother so that the two could make up for lost time.

And Kim wanted to do more. In 2012, a friend who fosters children told her that teenagers were the "lost generation" of the system, as everyone wants the endearing young children but not the rebellious teens. Kim prayed on it. She did some research. She considered where she had started and where she was now. She knew what it was like to be lost, and she decided that she wanted to help members of the lost generation.

"I may not be able to reach the world," she says, "but I can reach one."

Specifically, she wanted to foster teenage girls. She told Indy it would be a blessing, and she became a foster parent.

"I just said, 'Lord, teach me to love,'" she recalls. "He had to show me through His goodness and kindness, and through that, you start to develop the character of God."

It worked out well, even if it created some interesting moments for Indy. One day in high school, a girl was sitting behind her in English class. The next day, she was living with her.

The Lord had one more blessing for Kim.

As a foster mom, she needed a bigger house, and she had

her eye on an empty, dilapidated blue house on the very street on which she was living. It was on an acre of land, with two stories, a basement, and three bedrooms. Across the street from Perry High School, it was mainly used by teenagers to smoke and drink. Kim would walk down the street, look in the dusty windows, and say, "This is my house."

She spoke to God about it—but Indy, now in high school, spoke to a real estate agent. It turned out that the house was owned by Bank of America, but Habitat for Humanity had agreed to gut it and renovate it. Kim spoke to the organization and explained how she wanted to buy the house so that she had more room to foster children. The bank gave her an interest-free loan, and Habitat volunteers rehabbed it. It certainly felt like a miracle. And in 2012, Kim rented a tiny U-Haul, loaded her belongings, and moved down the street. Not everything fit, so she strapped her mattress to the top of her car and rolled that down the street as well.

Kim likes to quote something that Joyce Meyer, a Christian author, often says: "You can't be pitiful and powerful at the same time." In other words, you must shed your pitiful excuses if you're going to power through this life. You can't be both a victim and a fighter. You must choose. Kim chose to be a fighter.

And in my case, she also chose to be a believer.

CHAPTER 14
A TEST OF WILLS

MISS KIM saw part of her former self in me—the belligerence, the rebellion, the aimlessness. Just like her, I had succumbed to temptations that I shouldn't have. Just like her, I had thought about suicide and had even made clumsy attempts. And just like her, I had reached such a low point that I didn't give a damn what happened next to me.

My caseworker was skeptical that Miss Kim would bring me into her home, because Miss Kim only fostered girls. But the caseworker had no other options, and Miss Kim reassured her that this was meant to me. "God has a plan," she told her.

Before she brought me into her home, she said a prayer:

> *Father God, we have a situation where they want this young boy to come into our home. Father, you always know the end from the beginning. Everything is divine in your will and in your plan, and if it's purposeful for this child to be here, Father God, I ask that you give me wisdom, give me insight, Lord God, so I can be a vessel, Lord God, so I can be a part of this child's life.*
>
> *Father God, I just ask that you bind your will to whatever purpose that you have for him, because you said in your word that whatever we bind on earth will be bound in heaven.*

She thought I just hadn't been with the right family. "Water is good in its element," she tells me. "It hydrates us. It makes plants grow. And electricity is good in its element. It gives us light. It charges our cell phones. But if you put water and electricity together, you've got something deadly."

My other foster parents and I, she concluded, were like water and electricity, and she was going to make up her own mind. "You're not who these people say you are," she once told me. "You're who God says you are."

Right after New Year's 2015, when I was seventeen, I moved into Miss Kim's renovated house, and it felt good to be in a stable neighborhood. No more gunshots. No more sirens. I'd sit on the back patio, smoking a blunt, a police car would drive by, and I'd wave.

I had my own room, so it felt like I was living in a mansion. Indy also lived there. On the cusp of emancipation, I was obviously grateful for this new start, but I was also hesitant to embrace it—a reaction, I think, to all the things that had gone wrong at other homes. But Miss Kim's entire family—including both her daughters, her brothers, her cousins, and her parents—accepted me.

Miss Kim's faith in God not only gave her strength to bring me into her family, but, I believe, it also allowed her to see me for who I really was and not as someone who was supposed to behave in a certain way, and not the "problem kid" that my file said I was. All my other foster parents wanted me to wear my prosthetics. I'm supposed to have legs because we all have legs. That was their thinking, and that's what school officials, with the exception of Coach Donahue, wanted me to do as well.

My prosthetics once served a purpose, to help my spine, but my back was now healthy. My prosthetics were now just about conforming to society and minimizing the stares from people who didn't know what to make of a person without legs. But I wanted to look like myself. I didn't want to conform. Why take away my being on the ground, which is what I'm used to, and put me higher, which I don't like?

I was in constant rebellion against those fake legs and against society's expectations of what I was supposed to look and act like.

Shortly after I moved in with Miss Kim, she said to me, "Zion, you have to wear your prosthetics."

"I don't like wearing them," I said.

"Why?"

"Because they're ugly and they're uncomfortable, and I like walking on my hands, and you're not the one who has to wear them."

"Fine," she said. "Don't wear them, then."

She understood who and what I was, and those damn legs have been in her basement ever since.

From day one, Miss Kim was impressed with how easily I moved around her house, preparing my own food, using my long reach and my leaping ability to gain access to whatever I needed, though not everything went as planned. To brush my teeth, I jumped on the bathroom countertop and accidentally yanked it out of the wall. That's when she started calling me "Little Hercules."

She treated me like I was one of her own children, which meant both love and discipline. For the last three years, at Mrs. Kirkland's house, I would come and go as I pleased and hang out with whomever I wanted. No more. Now when I wanted to go to someone's house, Miss Kim would only let me go if she knew the parents.

"But they're having a party," I said, "and everyone is going to be there."

"Everyone isn't going to be there," she said, "because you ain't going to be there."

Once when I missed curfew, she grounded me for three days and had me do extra chores. She also told me that I was running with the wrong crowd, and they weren't coming into her house.

"You ain't my mom!" I shouted.

That hurt her, but she wasn't deterred. If I didn't come home when I was supposed to, she'd go to where I was, knock on the door, and get me. "If I allow you to do this," she said, "I'm no better than the next person."

I wasn't ready for that type of discipline. I was still defiant, unruly, still had the ghetto mindset. I had been living with Miss Kim for about six weeks when late one afternoon, we got into an argument and I just walked out of her house. "I'm going to call the police," she yelled as I stalked out.

I was on Lincoln Way, heading toward Canton, when a police car pulled up next to me.

"Are you Zion?"

"Fuck off!" I said.

"Don't talk to me that way."

"Fuck off, pig! I ain't going with you."

That's how the gangbangers talked to cops. They were the enemy.

"You can either get in my car, and I'll take you back to your mom's house, or if you do anything besides that, I can take you to the jail."

I looked at him, smiled, and bolted. I hopped three fences and hid in a trash can. I don't know how long I was there, but I realized that this was useless. I couldn't hide in a trash can the rest of my life, and I wasn't in a bad part of town anymore. I went back to the road, sat on the curb, and waited until the cop drove by and picked me up. They took me to the station but dropped all charges. Miss Kim came and took me home, then grounded me for two weeks.

It was a test of wills, in which I would try to break some rule (going to a party I shouldn't be at, bringing home a girlfriend), and Miss Kim would usually discover it. She said I was trying to "outslick" her, "but you can't outslick a can of oil."

One time, she was so angry with me—I believe it was for getting into a fight at school—that she told me to leave the house, even though it was one a.m. "Don't come back for a while," she said.

I slammed the door, which I wasn't allowed to do. It was cold, and I asked to come back in.

"No. You can come back tomorrow."

She needed to blow off steam. So did I. So I got in my wheelchair and pushed myself through downtown Massillon, parts of which are uphill, to Kelcey's house. It's five miles, and my fingers were frozen by the time I arrived. But I knew I was always welcome there, and her mom—my second mom—was still up baking her cakes in the kitchen.

"I can't go home tonight," I told her.

"That's fine," Stefanie told me. "You can stay here."

She texted Miss Kim and told her that I was at her house and that I was safe.

I slept on a couch, and Stefanie took me home the following day.

For all our battles, I knew Miss Kim was doing it out of love. In word and deed, she showed me that. Because so much of my life had been defined by losses, she wanted me to believe in myself. "'Can't' is a cussword in this house," she told me, "because if you say you 'can't,' you won't. And if you can't do something, don't ever say that. Just say, 'I haven't learned that yet.'"

She saw how other people looked at me when I played sports, like I was a freak, and she said to me, "If they're going to look at you, give them something to remember."

Because she got into fights when she was young, she was a bit more lenient when I lost my temper, and she wanted me to stand up for myself. As a senior in high school, I was getting bullied by this one kid, who spat on my desk. So I punched him and broke his glasses. I was sent to the principal, who said, "I'm going to call your mom."

I said, "I'll call my mom!"

The principal told Miss Kim what happened, but she wasn't mad at me. "If someone had done that to me," she told me, "I would have done the same thing—but not on school property."

I thought I had certain talents in sports, music, and art, but Miss Kim made sure I understood the difference between talent and character. Quoting Bishop T. D. Jakes, she told me, "Your talents will carry you where your character can't keep you."

I could be the best wrestler or musician or artist in the world, but if my character is poor, my success won't last.

After I had been living with Miss Kim for five months, I felt that we had hit a groove, but then I came home from school and found my caseworker there.

Oh, no, I thought. *What have I done now? Where will I be headed?*

The three of us sat down in the living room, and Miss Kim said, "You know, your sisters love you, your uncles love you, and I love you as if I birthed you. Our whole family is in love with you."

She paused and then said: "Can I be your mother?"

I was shocked! I was also scared. She wasn't the first foster parent who'd expressed interest in adopting me. I didn't know if I could trust her, and I told her I would need to think about it.

Miss Kim did a lot of praying, and I spoke to Kelcey, who could already see how much I had changed since moving in with Miss Kim. "It looks like you're not angry at the world anymore," she said. About a week passed, and then I came home on a Friday and said, "Miss Kim, I need to talk to you."

We sat down, and it felt as if some higher power had taken over my body.

"I would love if you were my mother," I said.

We both burst into tears. I can't say why or how I overcame my fears over the course of that week. Living with Miss Kim just felt right.

"What are you going to call me?" she asked, wiping her eyes.

"Mom," I said confidently.

We had to go to court to file the paperwork and get my

name changed, but there was confusion about what day in June we were due. I was in school when my caseworker called the front office. A staff member got me out of class, and we made a beeline downtown. It was a hot day, and Miss Kim was waiting for me at the courthouse. Someone was screaming, "Where is Zion? Where is Zion?" when I came running in on my hands, wearing gym shorts and a torn wrestling shirt. Miss Kim and I stood before Judge Dixie Park, who has dark straight hair and bangs and was looking so official in her dark robe and white collar. Both Miss Kim and I were sweaty and out of breath, and I can barely remember what Judge Park said. What I do recall is that at the end of her remarks, she looked at my mom and said, "That's your son. You can hug your son now." And she did.

I was seventeen, just three months before I turned eighteen—twelve weeks before my emancipation.

I took my mom's maiden name and was now Zion Clark.

CHAPTER 15
THE JACKPOT OF OTHERNESS

I HAD BEEN part of the Ohio foster care system for most of my life, but for all my complaints about it, I didn't know the half of it. Only later did I discover that in addition to providing me with questionable care for the majority of my childhood, the state of Ohio also withheld money from me.

By the time I was born, in 1997, a federal law was in place designed to help kids like me with the financial fallout of our unique circumstances. According to the law, any young person in foster care, regardless of age, is entitled to Social Security benefits if that young person has a significant mental or physical disability or if that child has a parent who died. Under those criteria, about 10 percent of foster kids, out of four hundred thousand in the system nationwide, are eligible for these benefits.

The kids, of course, have no way of applying for their money. They're too young. Even as older teenagers, they probably can't do it because they don't know the law exists. They have no advocates. Instead, the states are supposed to determine which children are eligible and then sign them up for benefits, and those benefits—cash payments—are supposed to accrue to the child.

I only found out about this law in 2021, through an investigation by NPR and the Marshall Project (a nonprofit that focuses on criminal justice). The reports revealed that "state foster care agencies routinely take the Social Security benefits from the youth in their care—at least $165 million a year." According to the reports, cash payments are typically more than seven hundred dollars a month per beneficiary.

That's a lot of money, but I didn't know about it and never saw any of it since the payments went to Stark County.

The rationale behind the law is obvious. Even under ideal circumstances, foster kids who age out of the system have higher rates of poverty, homelessness, and mental health problems, and the kids with significant disabilities or whose biological parent or parents have died face even greater hardships. The Social Security payments, as they accrue during the years in which that child is in the system, provide a financial buffer against those hardships.

But the states, including Ohio, keep the money for

themselves on the grounds that it helps offset the costs of running the foster care system in the first place. In 2003, the US Supreme Court, in a suit brought by a family in Washington State, effectively agreed with the states that it was lawful to keep the money intended for foster youth, but the ruling left numerous questions unresolved. Another lawsuit, demanding that the state of Alaska pay foster children their Social Security benefits, is now working its way through the courts.

I was in the Ohio foster care system for about sixteen years. Assuming a conservative benefit payment of seven hundred dollars a month, I should have received $134,400 upon Miss Kim's adoption of me, which ended my time in the system. My total would be much higher if the money had been placed in a simple interest-bearing account and appreciated over time.

But I didn't receive a nickel.

Responding to a question about these payments, Robert Myers, deputy director of the Children Services Division for Stark County Job & Family Services, wrote in an email: "As a [public children's services agency] we are allowed to use benefits as a means to partially offset some of the costs directly related to the care and placement of a child. . . . It is similar, if not the same, as how a parent would use the benefit to cover the needs of their child."

But it is *not similar*, and it is in *no way the same*. Stark County was never my actual parent. It's a government agency that is responsible for providing foster care services funded by local and state tax dollars. Stark County, along with counties and states across the country, is asking kids like me to pay for our own foster care services. As Daniel L. Hatcher, a law professor at the University of Baltimore, told NPR and the Marshall Project, government officials "don't even realize that this is not just another funding stream—this is literally the children's own money. This is about whether we are going to use abused and neglected children's own money to pay for what we're supposed to be providing them as a society."

That's exactly how we are using this money, and I believe it's because kids in general, but particularly foster kids, are easy to exploit. We don't have power. We don't have resources. We aren't allowed to vote. And when we do speak up, people don't listen to us or don't believe us.

I suppose it's fitting that I didn't receive my Social Security benefits, because if it's possible for one person to expose all the faults of a broken foster care system, it's probably me. And those faults, common across the country, have been documented in Ohio. In 2019, Governor Mike DeWine established a commission to investigate the state's foster system, and a preliminary report in February 2020 said that of the more than sixteen thousand children who are in custody of a children's services agency, almost 10 percent "receive repeat incidents of child maltreatment within one year."

Those children who are in the home of a "kinship caregiver" do pretty well, but those in regular foster care? Not so good. According to the preliminary report, "Along with the trauma children experience when they are removed [from family], research shows that most children in foster care have experienced ongoing or complex trauma, which has significant, often lifelong, negative effects on brain development, relationship-building, and physical and mental health."

How any of us survive is a wonder.

The children who are removed from their homes and then reunited certainly face upheaval and perhaps emotional injury, but at least family stability is restored. There are many kids, however, without families or without support networks, solid communities, or dependable social services. We're the unwanted children in a land of wealth and privilege, the visible reminders of systemic breakdowns: of families, of neighborhoods, and of government agencies that are supposed to protect children.

Confronted by so much failure, most Americans, I believe, simply recoil and look away. The plight of unwanted children is too overwhelming for most people to confront, and I was more overwhelming than most—the jackpot of otherness. I embodied what our country cannot acknowledge or reconcile.

Revelations about the foster care system, for me, came from unexpected places, even down the street.

My mom lived on the same street, Fairlawn Avenue SW, as the Sparkman family—Joshua and Diana, their sons, Casey and Darese, and their daughter, Destiny. The two boys, several years apart, were championship wrestlers at Perry High School and wrestled in college. I was between them in age, and Casey was in college by the time I moved onto Fairlawn. The three of us worked out together that summer before my senior year.

The Sparkmans were one of the few intact families with whom I spent significant time and where I felt wanted. I went to their home on Father's Day just to see how it was done. In some ways, my most important friendship with the family was with Mrs. Sparkman. She was a good cook, so that was an added incentive to spend time at the house and gave me many opportunities to speak with her. Half Black, half Puerto Rican, she also grew up in foster homes, and she understood me in ways that few in the community did.

The foster home experience leaves a mark on every child who goes through it, and Mrs. Sparkman spoke candidly about her experiences (and told me I could share them in this book).

Many foster parents, she said, should have never gotten the job. "When you become a foster parent, you're sacrificing a piece of your life," she told me. "But if you're not willing to do that, you have no right invading these kids' lives."

She had been abused as a foster child, and I told her about my experiences. "I understand exactly where you're coming from," she said. "I understand how it feels to want to be loved so bad, and you just get abused. And that's what you learn—abuse." That abuse, she said, begins to feel normal, as if it's what you deserve. "It doesn't hit you like, 'This is not right. I don't deserve to be treated like that.'"

She told me that's why I had turned to the streets, because I never felt loved and didn't even think I deserved to be loved. She also told me that my disability made me even more vulnerable in the system. "At least I had legs," she said. "I could kick back."

Mrs. Sparkman was a bit like Kelcey's mother in that both were willing to share their vulnerabilities with me, and despite the setbacks and even traumas they had experienced, they each had strong families and had raised great kids and had good lives. That was particularly meaningful with Mrs. Sparkman, because she had survived foster care and was never adopted. (She was reunited with her biological parents.) All the years I was in foster care, I wanted to get adopted and feared aging out of the system before I ever had a mother or a father. Mrs. Sparkman made me realize that even if that happened to me, I could still make something of my life.

Sandy Schmucker, more than anyone I know, understands the foster care system, as she and her husband were part of it for four decades. The foster community in Stark County is small, and Mrs. Schmucker knows most of the other parents I lived with, either personally or by reputation. All these people brought me into their homes with the expectation of adopting me, but until Miss Kim came along, it never worked out.

Why?

Sandy Schmucker tells me that even among disabled children, I was a "novelty," not only because I had no legs but because I was spirited and had a big smile. Some of the parents who brought me in, she says, won a lot of praise for accepting someone with such a distinctive handicap. Who's ever heard of a kid with no legs who wrestles, plays the trumpet, and reads beyond his grade level? These parents were heroes in their own communities. “They got a lot of attention for it,” she says, “but when that started to wear off, it wasn’t fun anymore.”

Not for them, and certainly not for me.

CHAPTER 16
SUPERHERO IN A SINGLET

MOVING IN WITH MY MOM, even before she became my mom, yielded immediate benefits. I got off the streets and stopped running with the wrong kids. I also improved in the classroom, as I simply had better focus and fewer worries. My grades had been tanking, but I pulled them up and finished my junior year with all my coursework completed.

I didn't play in the band my senior year but found another option.

Massillon High School has several different choirs, and in my senior year, I auditioned to play the drums for the Washingtonians, which drew students interested in musical theater and singing. Until now, I had just played the drums for my own enjoyment, but I tried out for the Washingtonians and was chosen to be its drummer. The group had about twenty members, with the boys wearing rose-colored vests and bow ties and the girls wearing dresses in the same color. We played at community events and performed such numbers as "Let It Go," from the movie *Frozen,* and Pharrell Williams's song "Happy."

That put me on the right musical foot for my senior year. Then there was wrestling.

For all the turmoil in my life, I never gave up on wrestling. It was the only way that I could channel my rage productively, without getting into trouble, but whatever emotional value the sport had was short-lived because I always lost. My disadvantage was obvious, but it wasn't just that I didn't have legs. I always weighed less than my opponents. Even at fifteen as a high school freshman, I only weighed eighty pounds, and the lightest weight class was 106 pounds. I didn't have the size, strength, or skill to be competitive. I also didn't have the mindset and the focus. All I had was exhaustion from defeat.

Coach Donahue and Coach McGhee felt my losses as deeply as I did, but they were also bulwarks against my frustration. Fearing that I would quit, Coach Donahue once said to me, "We won't let you walk out of this room."

I'm the same age as Coach Donahue's son, Jake, who was also a wrestler, and a really good one. Coach Donahue had seen many of my matches in middle school while watching his son. In his view, I was like a car with no back wheels, trying to propel the vehicle forward while dragging the rear on the ground. I had no power underneath, no propulsion. While I lost match after match, I was rarely pinned. I always battled, always scrapped. I had enough strength in my arms and back, and enough agility, to survive the entire match. But I had no leverage to actually win. Or, like a car with no back wheels, I was perpetually stuck in a ditch.

Coach Donahue and I would often spar, though it wasn't always planned. We had scrimmages in which my opponent refused to take the mat against me. I'd walk off and tell Coach Donahue, "Nobody wants to wrestle me."

"Don't worry, Zion. I got you."

So I'd scrimmage against Coach.

We even had meets in which the other guy would weigh in but not take the mat and forfeit. I never counted those as wins.

In sparring with me, Coach Donahue discovered that I had one advantage: my grip. My years of walking on my hands had given me uncommon strength in my hands and arms—sort of like a Marvel superhero's special attribute. Once I grab someone's wrist, I can hold it and bruise it or even break it. But I still couldn't overcome my liabilities. Any time my opponent got under one of my arms and pushed me, I had no way to repel him.

Even worse is the basic structure of the sport. The first period begins with wrestlers in the neutral position, facing each other on their feet. The second and third periods begin with one wrestler on top and the other on bottom, on hands and knees. The bottom wrestler can escape by shooting out his legs. Well, since I have no legs, I got killed every time I was on bottom. I wasn't that great on top either, because I lacked leverage. I was best in the neutral position, which was used for only one of three periods.

As a freshman and sophomore, wrestling on the junior varsity, I lost all my matches. In many of them, though, I was leading at the end of the first period. Then the next two periods, starting on bottom or top, I'd fall behind and lose. What I hated most were the tournaments, in which once I'd lose, I'd have to watch the rest of the match from the stands. I was supposed to cheer my teammates, which I did, but I didn't want to be in the stands anymore. I wanted to be on the mat.

My despair mounted, and I'd asked Coach Donahue, "What do I have to do to win? What do I have to do to raise my hand?"

He wanted me to win as much as I did. When we traveled to a meet, the school required me to bring my wheelchair and to use it to get from the bus to the gym. But I didn't want to enter any gym in a damn wheelchair. I wanted to walk, but the ground was too cold and slippery for my hands. So Coach Donahue would put me on his shoulders, and he carried me into gyms across Ohio. In size and weight, he compared me, affectionately, to a knapsack.

We tried different moves in practice, all trial and error, but nothing worked. Coach Donahue had never even seen a wrestler without legs, so he had to find a different way to teach me. He lay awake at night trying to figure it out. Then he had an idea.

The rules of wrestling effectively discriminate against the disabled athlete by requiring that athlete to assume the top or bottom position in the second and third periods. But why should the disabled athlete have to accommodate the abled world instead of the other way around? Why can't the rules be changed so it's fair for everyone?

Coach Donahue wrote a letter to Beau Rugg, who oversaw officiating for the Ohio High School Athletic Association. Coach said he had a wrestler without legs who was winning many of his matches but would then lose once he had to take the top or bottom position. He said it wasn't fair, and his wrestler should be able to start each period in the neutral position. He also sent Rugg a video of me wrestling and followed up with a phone call.

I assume this was the first time that Rugg had ever had such a request, and to his credit, he agreed. Starting my junior year, I began each period in the neutral position.

That helped, but Coach Donahue and I still had to reinvent the sport, trying to figure out what moves I could use. He told me not to reach my arm up high, because if my opponent gets under my arm, he can drive me back and it's over. Coach McGhee told me I had to keep my chin over my belly button so that I'd maintain my balance. The key was exploiting my greatest strength, my grip. But I needed to use my grip in a conventional wrestling move, and I found the right one almost by accident.

Toward the end of my junior season, we had a tournament in Wheeling, West Virginia. Our 113-pound varsity wrestler injured himself, and the coaches suddenly put me in. I wrestled my tail off and won in overtime, and my arms were so tired, I couldn't walk off the mat. The coaches had to carry me back to the bench.

But it was how I won—the move that I used—that made all the difference and gave me new hope.

The Peterson roll sounds like something you'd order in a deli, but it was one of the few wrestling moves that I could execute. It required, however, that I set a trap: make my opponent believe he was in command, then turn the tables, or roll him on his back.

Here's how it was executed: When my opponent was on top of me, I'd use my right hand to grab his right wrist and pin it hard against my waist. I'd then roll left, and with my forehead on the mat and my butt in the air, I'd use my left arm to reach through his legs and hook his right thigh. Then I'd roll over and reverse him, while still gripping his wrist like a vise. Finally, I'd lean back on him and get the points or even the pin.

One moment, he was on top of me, and then—*bam!*—he was on his back. It was fast, it was lethal, and it worked.

The Peterson requires explosive quickness and precise timing, and once I realized I could do it, I must have practiced it on Coach Donahue a thousand times. He weighed 145 pounds, so he was way above my weight class. But that just made me better.

I also practiced on Karson, Kelcey's little brother. Karson was a wrestler, and even though he was younger, we had some good battles in the basement. One day I hit him with my move, and he yelled up to his mom, "Zion Petersoned me!"

I practiced and perfected a similar move called the tilt, but I always had more to learn. In my junior year, I was winning a match when my opponent put me in a quarter nelson. I didn't know how to defend it because we had never practiced it. I was pinned and lost. I was ticked off and asked Coach Donahue how I was supposed to win if I didn't know how to counter these moves?

He taught me the move during our next practice, and I never lost a match by a quarter nelson again.

My victory in Wheeling gave me momentum going into the off-season that summer of 2015. My goal hadn't changed. I wanted to win every match. I wanted to be great. I wanted to make the state finals. I wanted to be a superhero in a singlet. Which may have seemed hilarious, given that after three years, I still wasn't good enough to make varsity. And for all the power in my arms and hands, I was still a gaunt eighty-two pounds. But I was committed, and starting that summer, I devoted my whole life to increasing my strength and stamina.

My mom worked during the day, so I'd push my

wheelchair three miles up Lincoln Way to Massillon High School, where Coach McGhee ran the summer workouts.

Coach McGhee was even more intense and more demanding than Coach Donahue; by his own reckoning, he was the "bad cop" to Coach Donahue's "good cop." After the team wrestled poorly in one tournament, the next day in practice, he put us through two and a half hours of nonstop movement, not even a water break. "No one's going to feel sorry for you!" he'd tell us. He pushed kids so hard, they would sometimes cry, but he'd cry with them and embrace them. His day job was working in juvenile corrections, so he dealt with all kinds of kids who ended up in jail. He was also biracial, identifying as Black, and he grew up in a mostly white community in southern Ohio. He knew that he had to be better just to be good enough—that the people in his town were not just going to let any Black boy take something from a white boy. And that's what he taught all his wrestlers, regardless of race: you have to be better just to be good enough.

I did a lot of drilling that summer, but Coach McGhee also designed specific drills for me. He stacked wrestling mats over my head, and I had to climb them, up and down, up and down. I also did, on any given day, hundreds of dips, pull-ups, and burpees, as well as weightlifting, which was always a challenge. The barbells were fine, but I couldn't bench-press because I couldn't keep my torso on the bench. The coaches tried to strap me down, but I didn't like that. Finally, Coach

McGhee simply held me down, and I was able to increase my benching from 120 to 225 pounds. He also put me through drills on the mat with weights around my arms to increase their strength and explosiveness.

After my workout at Massillon High School, I'd push my wheelchair back down Lincoln Way to Perry High School, close to my house, and I'd go to the Perry gym. Perry was always a wrestling powerhouse, so I would spar there with some of the toughest wrestlers in the region.

Both workouts combined, I'd wrestle four or five hours a day, then I'd come home, change, and go for a run on my hands.

By the time I got back, I'd be so tired that sometimes I'd fall asleep at the base of the stairs.

I got bigger, increasing my weight to eighty-eight pounds, which helped me on the mat but also created challenges. My upper body was growing, but my feet remained underdeveloped. My right foot, the one I can control, is one long bone, and sometimes I would land on it wrong while wrestling, and I could feel the bone bending but not breaking. This happened three different times, and it was the worst pain I've ever felt.

Nonetheless, I was slowly developing a competitor's physique. That summer before my senior year, I got into a pull-up contest with my friend Casey Sparkman. He's a couple years older than I am, and a stud. His senior year in high school, wrestling at 152 pounds, he was a state champion with a 51–5 record, and after that, he won more than a hundred matches in four seasons at Kent State.

I still thought I could do more pull-ups. We started at the same time, but once we hit twenty, my arms began to tire, my palms were sweaty, and I could no longer hang on. I dropped to the floor, and Casey kept going. He gave me a hard time about it, too.

A year later, we were working out again, but by now I had built myself up. I challenged him to a rematch, and this time I didn't get tired. Casey wore down, and when he let go of the bar, I kept going and yelled at him, "Is that all you got?" I did about fifteen more pull-ups before I dropped to the ground.

If my physical well-being improved when I moved in with my mom, so, too, did my spiritual well-being. I had gone to church when I lived with Granny, and her devoutness left its mark. But it was hard for me to keep my faith. More than once, in some of the homes I was in, I thought, *What kind of God would allow this to happen?* I knew that I wasn't always living up to God's expectations, and I didn't particularly like going to church every Sunday. I thought other people were jamming faith down my throat instead of making it enjoyable. I was at my spiritual low point when I left Mrs. Kirkland's house—at the time, I didn't care about anything, including God.

That didn't sit well with my mom, who wanted me to go to church every week. I resisted, and we argued about it. She thought I was denying God, but I wanted to praise Him in my own way. You don't have to go to church to be a faithful man. You don't have to go to Bible class every Wednesday to be a God-fearing man.

My mom stopped insisting that I go to church, ending those arguments. But a funny thing happened. It was through her that I saw faith in action—whenever she helps another human being or when she helps the schools, her church, or her family. She does so because she knows that is what God wants of her. For all the adversity in her life, she believes the answers to this troubled world can be found in God, and it was through her faith that she found a much better life than she could have ever imagined. That was a powerful lesson for me.

I started reading the Bible on my own, and I kept it in my backpack and carried it with me wherever I went. I do that to this day, and I always find passages, some familiar, some new, that speak to me—about abandonment and disability, prejudice and perseverance. And these passages will speak to me for the rest of my life.

I still don't go to church very often, but I have my mom to thank for reawakening me to His presence. She just pours out endless amounts of love to her friends and family and community. And she does the same for me, even when I'm wrong. That is not just her. That is God.

CHAPTER 17
PIN TO WIN

WRESTLING PRACTICES during my senior year began formally in October. We were supposed to be on the mat each afternoon at 3:30 p.m., but a lot of guys would start drilling at 2:30. We taped our hands, stuck in our mouthpieces, and got ready quickly. The wrestling room had padded walls, no windows, and was about eighty degrees. While the other wrestlers did repeated wind sprints and various exercises that I couldn't do, the coaches developed a special workout for me. They called it a cage—it was just an enclosed space surrounded by a net—and they created a circuit for me: do twenty-five push-ups and twenty-five burpees, leap onto a stack of mats, jump down, run three wind sprints . . . and repeat.

I'd do that circuit until they told me to stop.

We'd spar at 4:45, and if someone was not working hard, the coaches would stop the practice and make everyone do push-ups. By 5:15, everyone was drenched, and then we'd play a game like "bull in the ring," in which you might wrestle eighteen straight minutes, or mat hockey, in which we used a taped ball as a puck and played a combo wrestling/hockey game. That was fun, and the coaches had to apologize to the parents who were waiting to pick up their kids while we were busy smashing into each other inside.

. . .

I finally made varsity, and I knew that I had the respect of my teammates: they voted me one of the captains, and that meant a lot. But could I win any matches? Or would I just be a circus act who drew media attention?

I didn't know. I was glad to be up to eighty-eight pounds, but even competing at the lowest weight class, I was still eighteen pounds lighter than every opponent.

Our high school had televisions in each classroom, and we had our own channel run by students. Each day in second period, the televisions were turned on, and the students who worked at the channel broadcast daily announcements. These often included news about Massillon sports—the results from the previous day, the schedule for the day coming up, which players had excelled. It was a big deal to get your name called out.

My senior year, our opening wrestling meet was against McKinley, and that day the student on the Massillon channel wished us well against our rival. The wrestlers wore coats and ties on the days of all our meets, a tradition. My last class was in construction trades, and about half the class were wrestlers. It was steaming hot, and we were allowed to take off our jackets. I was anxious and was just trying to focus on the match and the different ways it could go.

Because I wrestled at the lowest weight, I was in the first match, and that meant I had to set the tone. Prior to entering the gym, the team gathered in the locker room, and I stood in the middle. Coach Donahue began with a prayer, another tradition.

"God, please watch over our wrestlers. Keep them safe from injury and let them wrestle to the best of their ability."

He reminded us how hard we had worked, how we deserved it, and what it meant to represent our school and our community.

I led the final cheer: "One! Two! Three! Pin to win!"

I raced into the gym, my teammates trailing behind me.

Before my match began, Coach Donahue told me, "I've only lost to these guys once. I don't want to lose to them now."

That was always the mindset against our rival:

GO HARD OR GO HOME.

I was in my own world. I also had my routine before each match. I meditated. I sucked a lime to jolt my body. I dabbed a finger in honey and licked it to give me a slight sugar rush. I put on my gloves and got ready.

Then I saw something that made me realize this match really was different. My mom was in the crowd, and she was impossible to miss.

"Give me a *Z*! Give me an *I*! Give me an *O*! Give me an *N*!"

I'd been wrestling for most of my life, but she was the first person to show up and cheer me on. For many kids who play sports, their parents are there all the time, and some kids would beg their parents—the dreaded soccer moms—not to show up. But if you've never had a parent at one of your games when all the other kids have theirs, and those parents are cheering like crazy and no one is cheering for you, let me tell you: it hurts. The gyms themselves are relatively small, and a wrestling match may only get a hundred fans; so even one boisterous fan can be heard. And now I had my fan, and I was not going to let her down.

The match began. My style was ankle-picking and head-butting, and in the first ten seconds, I took my first shot and took him down. In years past, even when I got the first take-down, my opponent could usually overpower me, escape, turn me, and get on top. But not this time. Every time he tried to stand up, I'd grab him and drag him back down. I was too strong—at least much stronger than he was, and much stronger than I'd ever been before. I rode him for forty-five seconds. I knew he was finished by the end of the first period, and I molly-whopped him for six minutes.

At the end, the referee raised my hand while my mom stood and cheered. The following day, during second period, the student reading the daily announcements said that Massillon had defeated McKinley in wrestling, and he named all the wrestlers who won their matches. Because mine was the first match, the first name he read was "Zion Clark."

I was just getting started.

About a month after the McKinley match, in the first week of January 2016, Massillon went to the J.C. Gorman tournament, one of the biggest in Ohio, and I beat two guys who were ranked. Reporters came up to Coach Donahue and said, "Hey! This guy doesn't have any legs." They asked how I could win at wrestling.

"I saw it coming years ago," he said.

I won my first twelve matches, and the student broadcaster started referring to me as "the undefeated Zion Clark!"

Other kids came up to me and said, "You're good now."

"I'm just working hard," I replied.

I finally lost a match and then won eight more. I also provided some comic relief. After one match in Canton, we were getting dressed in the locker room, and a water pipe broke. Suddenly, hot water and steam came pouring into the room, so we all started running out. But I had a hard time getting traction with my hands, and I hit a slick spot, fell backward, and slid right on my back across the floor. Everyone cracked up, and so I did I.

As I got better, my opponents didn't know what to do. Some began backing out of the circle to stop play, which should have been a penalty for stalling and a point for me. But the referee never called it, apparently believing, now that I was stronger and faster, that I had the advantage because I was low to the ground.

Coach Donahue was always yelling at the referees, and one time, the ref turned to him and screamed, "Who's got the advantage here?"

Coach went ballistic. "The advantage? It's not my wrestler! He doesn't have any legs!"

As I won more, I did better in school, got into fewer scuffles, and seemed to have the respect of more kids. Maybe that's what happens when you excel in sports, or maybe I just didn't feel as if I had as much to prove.

My senior year in high school brought one other unexpected blessing.

One day I was online, and I received a message through Facebook from Shannon Kerr. At first, I didn't recognize the name, but I did once I read her note. I had met her six years ago with her adopted son—and my biological brother—Samuel. Miss Kerr said she had read about my wrestling and reached out to me. She said that she had called my previous foster home repeatedly and left messages, but my foster parents, the ones who were going to adopt me but backed out, never gave me those messages.

Incredible. I knew those foster parents could be cruel, but I never imagined they could be so cruel that they wouldn't want me to have a relationship with my brother. It was all the worse because Samuel and his mom had bought me a Christmas present the year that we met at McDonald's but were never able to give it to me.

Regardless, I was grateful to hear from Miss Kerr now, and we set up a time for Samuel and me to meet again. I also learned more about Samuel. We had more in common than having the same birth mother.

Like me, Samuel doesn't know who his father is. Like me, he doesn't have a relationship with our biological mother, and like me, he was born with significant medical challenges.

According to Miss Kerr, our birth mother "marinated in every street drug" during her pregnancy with Samuel. He was born five weeks premature, was addicted at birth to antipsychotic drugs, and was later diagnosed with fetal alcohol syndrome. There is no cure or treatment for fetal alcohol syndrome.

Samuel has cognitive deficits and little to no short-term memory, but with the help of a tutor and through many hours of hard work, he had advanced each year at his public school. Miss Kerr thought that if his biological mother hadn't taken drugs, he'd be a genius.

For our second get-together, in 2015, we met at the Carnation City Mall in Alliance, where the new Star Wars movie was showing. I was now eighteen, Samuel ten. We were just like two brothers having fun at the mall, with Samuel's mom in tow. We went to an arcade, and I won a rubber ball and gave it to Samuel. (I later found out that he kept it even after it popped.) We had our pictures taken with Darth Vader before the movie, then we got our popcorn and enjoyed the show. I had taken the bus there, but Miss Kerr drove me back home to Massillon, with my little brother.

CHAPTER 18
SUDDEN DEATH

THE GOAL of every high school wrestler is to make it to the state tournament. You want to win it, of course, but to say that you "went to state" is a badge of honor for the rest of your life. In Ohio, wrestlers first enter a sectional tournament, and if they place in the top four in their weight class, they go to the district tournament. There, each weight class has sixteen participants, and the top four advance to state, where each weight class has sixteen more participants. No sport puts its athletes through the gauntlet like wrestling.

In February 2016, I won three out of four matches at sectionals, which qualified me for districts in the 106-pound division. I was one of five wrestlers from Massillon to qualify, and though I had a good record, 31–14, I wasn't ranked and entered every match at districts as an underdog. The teams in sectionals were Division I schools, the biggest in Ohio, so I was competing against the best.

On Friday, February 26, a cold, overcast day, we took a school bus seventy-one miles to Mentor, a suburb of Cleveland, and stayed at a motel. The following day, we went to Mentor High School, home of the Fighting Cardinals and site of the district tournament. While most wrestling matches occur in relative obscurity, not so the district tournament. The large gym, draped with banners and flags, was packed with fans from all over the state. They sat shoulder to shoulder in the bleachers or stood on the sidelines, with the kids wearing their high school colors and their families the same. Unlike most sporting events, in which all eyes are trained on one competition, a district wrestling tournament has four matches running simultaneously, creating an electric environment. Whistles are blowing, not necessarily for your match but for a match one or two mats down. Coaches are yelling, fans are cheering, and the public address announcer can barely be heard above the din.

My mom was in the crowd. So were my two sisters, as well as Casey and Kelcey. Jake Donahue, the coach's son whom I'd known since middle school, was there competing in his own matches and watching all of mine, too. Coach Skelly was there. These were the people I cared about the most and who cared about me. I heard the noise, and sometimes I could even hear my fans cheering, but once the match began, all I cared about was whipping the guy across from me.

Virtually all my opponents were freshmen or sophomores, as 106 pounds is too low a weight for most upperclassmen. My first match was against a red-haired freshman from Solon named Jake Canitano; he dominated me and won 18–3. (He was also one of the better wrestlers of the era, finishing high school with a record of 150–15 and then going on to wrestle at Ohio State.) I won my next match and was waiting for my third opponent. Then I saw this guy walk onto the mat—he appeared to be from Walsh Jesuit High School, which was a wrestling factory, and I had heard the wrestler in my weight class, Hunter Olson, was one of the best in the state.

I asked Coach Donahue if that was Olson.

"Just go out there and wrestle," he told me. "It doesn't matter who they are."

It was Olson, and I beat him 13–7.

Forty-five minutes later, I would face Jack Gorman from Aurora. If I won, I'd go to state. If I lost, I'd go home, and my high school career would be over. I felt as though I had been working all year, indeed all my life, for this moment.

Gorman would be tough. He had begun wrestling in second grade, and now as a five-foot-two freshman, he had a record of 40–2. Practically unbeatable. I was exhausted, but I was still confident. I wasn't supposed to have gotten this far. I'd just beaten one of the top guys in the state, and I knew I could beat this guy as well.

Most wrestling matches have one referee. A district match has two to minimize officiating errors, and the lead referee wears two wristbands, one green and one red. Each wrestler is assigned a color so that when, say, the green wrestler scores a point, the ref's green wrist goes into the air.

I was red. Gorman was green.

Coach Donahue rubbed down my shoulders and sent me onto the mat. A wrestling mat consists of two concentric circles: the inner is where the match begins; the outer is the boundary. Gorman was waiting for me, standing almost frozen, in the center, while I bounded in on my hands. I was wearing my blue singlet with "Massillon" in orange across my chest, as well as an orange helmet. Gorman had a green singlet with a white stripe and a white helmet. I was much more muscular than he was—if you only saw us from the waist up, you'd think I had the advantage. Man against boy. But Gorman, of course, not only outweighed me but had length and leverage. I had strength and quickness.

We'd see who had the will.

I was still on the periphery when the ref walked into the center and leaned down. I ambled up to Gorman, and we shook hands. With that, the ref stepped back, and the match began.

Gorman immediately dropped to his knees, which signaled he knew what he was doing. Some of my opponents tried to wrestle me standing, but that gave me a bigger target and allowed me to grab their knees and take them down. My smart opponents knew they were better off tangling with me on their knees, at my level.

The first twenty seconds didn't see much action, which wasn't that unusual in my bouts. My opponents don't know what to make of me and have to figure out how to attack me, like deciphering some obscure computer code. But I had to do my own deciphering, as I tried to break through Gorman's defenses. I needed to understand how he was going to move and where he would apply pressure. I finally took a shot and grabbed his left leg. But I couldn't turn him, and he latched on to my left wrist. He was strong. We butted heads. I thrust forward and slammed his head onto the mat, but I still couldn't turn him. Neither of us was able to gain leverage, and the ref blew the whistle.

In any match, the ref wants action, so when opponents tie up, the ref calls a stalemate and has them separate and restart.

We returned to the center. This time, I danced around, though hardly in a conventional way. I lifted my feet up as well as my butt, and I swayed on my hands, with my singlet covering my feet and flopping to the ground. My feet were never visible on the mat. I looked like an optical illusion—or a Disney animation of half a body with twice the strength of a normal human being.

Except for me, it's just my regular movement.

We continued to butt heads until I grabbed Gorman's left wrist, but he thrust his right arm under my right arm to free himself. Move. Countermove. Move. Countermove. With seconds remaining in the first two-minute period, a teenager with a pink stick jogged up behind one of the refs. He is known as the "tapper," and when the clock reaches zero, he taps the ref on the back, who then blows the whistle. The ref can't watch the clock himself because his gaze must always be on the wrestlers.

The wrestlers don't see the tapper or the clock. We just battle until we hear the whistle.

Period one was over, and there was no score.

Period two began immediately, and it followed the same pattern. Gorman dropped to his knees, and I grabbed whichever wrist was on the ground. But I could never turn him, and neither could he turn me. About thirty seconds in, his left hand jammed my head, and his right hand grabbed my shoulder. Just as he was about to face-plant me, I cartwheeled backward to escape, my singlet flying into the air. It was an acrobatic move, and the crowd *ooh*ed.

Moments later, Gorman had his right hand around my head. I lunged for his leg, and he pushed my head down, thinking he could finally get on top. But my rear end flew up so that he had nothing to grab and control. The whistle blew, ending the second period. Still no score.

My body was fatigued. I felt it. But I believed that Gorman was even more tired, which motivated me. One more period before overtime, and I wanted to end it here. I started the period more aggressively, taking immediate shots at his legs and grabbing the back of his neck. But I still couldn't turn him, and he was equally tenacious, grabbing my wrists and trying to turn me. We disengaged, looked each other in the eye, and slammed into each other, head-to-head, like two angry bulls. I snared his left wrist, he clasped the back of my head, we fought and clawed, but again, neither of us could gain an advantage. After one scrum, we went out of bounds and had to restart. The seconds ticked down. The whistle blew. We were going into overtime.

The blood rounds.

The first overtime is one minute, and I'd begun to lose feeling in my hands and arms. We started, and Gorman got the early advantage, grabbing my left wrist and then using his left arm and both legs to push me onto the mat. His left arm was now around my neck, and he was on top of my shoulders. Every muscle ached, but I rolled onto my shoulder, shoved him with my left arm, and rolled out from under him. It's an explosive move. Coach Donahue and Coach McGhee, sitting courtside, started clapping, and someone in the crowd yelled, "Wow!"

As the seconds ticked down, I got beneath Gorman and grabbed his left leg, but I couldn't budge him, and we reached a stalemate. The first overtime ended with no points scored.

The rules change in the second overtime. Instead of starting in the neutral position, we had to start on top or bottom. I won the coin toss and chose bottom. In an overtime match during sectionals, I had chosen bottom and was able to escape, which earned me a point, so I thought I'd have a better chance on bottom. The period would last only thirty seconds, which may seem short, but for anyone wrestling, at this point it felt like an eternity.

Before the period started, Coach McGhee wiggled his body and said, "Granby," which is a roll I used to escape for my win in sectionals. But once the period started, Gorman inadvertently punched me in the mouth when he swiped his arm across my face. No quick Granby now. Gorman's left hand had my left arm, so I used my right arm to push up. If I could roll out, I'd get the point—but I couldn't, and he shoved each of his arms under my armpits and drove me down. I squirmed out and almost escaped, but he was soon back on top. He had both arms around my head, and my coaches were screaming, "Headlock! Headlock!" which is an illegal move. We stalemated instead, and the period ended as it began—scoreless.

Third overtime was the same structure, except now Gorman could choose top or bottom. He also chose bottom. He was on his knees, and I put my left arm around his stomach and my right hand on his right elbow. Right before the whistle, I rested my head on his back, and out of some combination of exhaustion and respect for a fellow warrior, I briefly closed my eyes.

The whistle blew. Gorman immediately stood and appeared certain to escape, but I grabbed his left ankle as he crawled away. I was hanging on, barely. I simply refused to let go—he was practically dragging me—but I moved my body into his and began to break him down. He may have had leverage on me, but no more. We were both on the ground, and I felt his strength ebbing.

My shoulder was in his stomach, and my left arm was around his right leg, my right arm around his left leg. I was trying to get leverage to execute the Peterson roll. Time was running short. I now had my right arm through his legs, gripping his right leg with all my power. All those hours in the gym had come down to this moment. He couldn't get out.

I used my left arm to push and—*BOOM!*—I spun and rolled him onto his back.

Just like the thousands of rolls we had done in practice.

Except it came a fraction of a second too late. The ref ruled that he had blown the whistle right before I completed the roll. The video later showed me executing the move *before* the tapper tapped the ref, but the video didn't capture the end of the roll. The call could have gone either way, but bottom line, I didn't do the move fast enough, which left it to the referee's judgment.

That's another thing Coach Donahue taught us: Don't let the ref decide a match. You decide it yourself.

Incredibly, by that point we'd wrestled three full periods and three overtimes, and not a single point had been scored.

The fourth overtime is called sudden death because whoever scores first wins. If no one scores, then the wrestler who started on top is given a point and declared the victor.

The ref tossed the coin to decide who would choose top or bottom. I won. I looked at my coaches, and they both said bottom. That meant that all Gorman had to do was ride me out, but it made sense. The last time I started on top, I was fortunate Gorman hadn't escaped. I was so weary, I doubt I could have prevented Gorman from just lifting himself up and walking away. And perhaps, starting on bottom, I'd have one Granby left in me.

The crowd had been loud throughout, but now they were on their feet cheering. Whatever matches they were watching before, they were now watching ours, a true epic battle.

I was beyond exhausted, and I felt as if my body was operating on its own. But I didn't care about the pain or the crowd or anything else. I just needed thirty seconds to find some way to escape.

We began the round, but my coaches were immediately on their feet screaming—the clock started early, so we had to begin again. Coach McGhee again yelled "Granby" at me, and the round started once more. I tried to push out, to roll, to maneuver, to do anything. But Gorman had his body on my body, both of his hands on my wrists, pressing hard, his legs giving him leverage. I couldn't get any traction. He wrapped his left arm around my body and continued to drive his torso against mine. The seconds ticked away. I squirmed and gained some distance, but he was right back on me. I used both my arms to push up, but he had me around the waist. The whistle blew. The ref raised his green wristband and his index finger: the green wrestler, Jack Gorman, had won one point, and the match.

After three blood rounds and a sudden death round, I'd been defeated.

Everyone in the stands was on their feet cheering. Other wrestlers were clapping. The refs were applauding. They had seen something they'd never seen before and would never see again.

I shook Gorman's hand and his coach's hand, and then I collapsed on the mat, in tears. Coach Donahue was crying as well, and he walked toward me, lifted me to his shoulder, and hoisted his right finger to the crowd—number one.

I didn't hear the cheers or even feel the presence of the fans. I simply felt broken, destroyed. I'm too competitive to take losing any other way. I've lost a lot of matches, but none hurt like this one. I sobbed into Coach Donahue's shoulder as he carried me out of the gym.

Jack Gorman placed in the state tournament (finishing in the top eight) and made it to state all four years in high school, where he won 139 matches.

Whoever filmed our match posted it on YouTube, and viewers can hear someone say, "Anybody thinks they have it rough should watch this video. This is amazing."

Coach Donahue had thought I lacked an identity, but now I had one. I was the kid who never gave up.

When a journalist later asked him what it had been like to coach me, he said, "I learned there is a God."

My high school wrestling career had ended, and looking back now, I take pride in my duel with Gorman. I had come so far to get to that crowded gym in Mentor, and on that one day, I discovered what my limits were. Ever since then, I have pushed myself to exceed them.

But wrestling, it turns out, wasn't the only sport in which I could excel.

CHAPTER 19
FOLLOWING IN MY FAMILY'S FOOTSTEPS

MY SISTER INDY is one of the best athletes I know. Regardless of the sport, she preferred competing against the boys, but in high school, she played on all-girls' teams in "powderpuff football." "Powderpuff" implies soft and feminine, but anyone who made contact with Indy—and she's only five foot one—usually ended up on her back.

Indy was a long jumper in track and field and was always a standout performer. But in 2015, her senior year, she missed the first part of the season because she had hurt her right knee in gymnastics over the winter. She only competed in five or six track meets but still reached the state finals in the long jump. The meet was held at Jesse Owens Memorial Stadium in Columbus, and I attended with my mom.

Even as a teenager, Indy was an old soul, always focused, stoic, and seeking ways to improve. Working with her track coach, Klifton Scott, she decided to add two more steps to her long jump for the state finals. Instead of taking twelve steps and leaping, she would take fourteen for greater speed. She practiced it for a week, but when she took her first jump at the finals, her timing was off, the jump was short, and it appeared the adjustment had backfired.

Each competitor got three jumps, and Coach Scott reassured Indy that she had done all the right things to prepare for this moment and that her next jump would be better.

If anyone could do it, I knew it was Indy. But on that next jump, she ran her fourteen steps, soared high, hit the sand, and then crumbled to the ground. She felt something pop in her right knee, and she couldn't move but now lay in tears. Coach Scott picked her up and carried her to a bench. He told her that her jump was good enough to win second place and that she didn't have to jump again.

"Second place is good," he said.

Not good enough for Indy.

She had missed the track finals the previous year because of an injury. She figured she was already hurt and had nothing to lose by jumping once more. There was no time to wrap her knee or do anything else to support it. When it was her turn, she hobbled to the starting line. To win, she needed to jump more than 18 feet, 3½ inches, but she had never jumped that far in her life. And off she went, fourteen steps, arms pumping, surging on adrenaline, and she sailed high and far, her palms skyward, then splashed into the sand with her usual authority.

Eighteen feet, 5½ inches. It was the longest jump of her life, and she won the championship.

We were all in tears.

There may be greater jumps or longer jumps in the history of high school track and field, but none that required as much courage. A few days later, Indy discovered that she made her championship jump with a torn MCL, a ligament on the inner knee.

Indy's sports career wasn't over. In the fall, she enrolled in the University of Akron, where she played rugby, and she also joined the National Guard.

Indy and I are truly brother and sister, and I was thrilled that she became a state champion. I was envious as well. She was Massillon's first state champion in any sport since 2011, and the city put up a banner in her honor across Lincoln Way and two signs on the highway.

I was completing my junior year in high school when Indy won her championship. I had never done anything in track and field, but I thought, *Man, I'd like to do something like that.* And I had one more year in high school to do it. The long jump wasn't possible, but there were other options.

After Indy's jump, I stayed to watch wheelchair racing, also known as seated racing. There I was, sitting in my own wheelchair, so I guess it's not surprising that a nice couple, Lisa and Brett Followay, walked up to me and introduced themselves. Their son, Casey, was born with spina bifida, causing paralysis in his legs. He'd been wheelchair racing all his life and really enjoyed it—he was a seven-time state champion. The Followays said they had seen me in the news for wrestling, and they thought I should try seated racing as well. They told me I had what it took to be good at it.

They were always trying to recruit new athletes into the movement. Casey had been a pioneer, racing since he was seven years old but also, with his parents, pushing for inclusion on his school track team. Not just to be *on* the team, in which he would careen around the track and everyone would cheer. He wanted to *contribute* to the team, and his parents convinced the Ohio track officials to adopt a scoring system that made that possible.

The Followays saw what racing did for Casey, so they started a nonprofit, Adaptive Sports Ohio, which promotes people with disabilities through sports. Its slogan captures every disabled athlete's most important goal: "A Chance to Play." Their efforts are all about making disabled athletes feel like part of society. Those of us with disabilities who live independent, fulfilling lives—drive our own cars, go to the grocery store, hold jobs—are seen as role models, but that's not enough. As Lisa says, "We're beyond the inspiration phase."

The Followays were not the first ones who urged me to take up seated racing. Coach Scott, the track coach, had been trying for the past three years.

Coach Scott knew me before I even reached high school. When I was in middle school, he saw me play soccer, using my hands as my feet to kick the ball. Once I was in high school, he brought me into his office at the start of each year and showed me videos of wheelchair racers. But I always said no. I was too invested in wrestling and the marching band. Then when I was at the state championship for Indy and the wheelchair racers had completed their race, Coach Scott walked up to me and said, "See? That's what I'm talking about."

With the encouragement of the Followays and Coach Scott, I decided to do it, but what really motivated me in seated racing was that I looked up to Indy. If she was a state champion, I wanted to be a state champion. If she was going to bring glory to our family name, I wanted to bring glory to our family name. I had just been adopted, and I now had these uncles and cousins who had been high school and college football stars and who had accepted me as their kin. I wanted to follow the trail that they had blazed. I wanted my new name to be in bright lights! So I joined the track team my senior year. Track didn't have the violence and beastliness of wrestling, so I couldn't hurt someone physically. But I could still hurt their feelings by beating them.

Problem was, neither Coach Scott nor I knew the first thing about wheelchair racing. We also didn't have a racing chair, which doesn't come cheap (they cost anywhere from three thousand to ten thousand dollars). My first several practices, I used my regular wheelchair as my racing chair. I would have looked like an idiot if I had to use it in an actual race, but

Coach Scott called Lisa Followay, and not only did her organization donate my first racing chair but she, Mr. Followay, and Casey personally delivered it to our school and gave me my first lesson. Mrs. Followay provided us guidance and support throughout the season. She knew that my upper-body strength gave me potential, and she also believes that when one disabled athlete has success—and that success is shared with the rest of the world—the entire community advances.

That's why she helped us so much that first season. As Coach Scott says, "She is literally an angel."

It turns out that I needed all the help I could get. I'd been pushing myself in a wheelchair my entire life, but wheelchair racing was completely different.

A regular wheelchair is all steel and aluminum and welded together, while a racing wheelchair is light and aerodynamic, made of carbon fiber, with two big wheels in back and one small wheel in front. You wear gloves, and in the seat you're actually on your knees, if you have knees. To propel the chair, your hands strike the rims of the back wheels. But you need to strike them in just the right spot, and let go at just the right time, to develop the rhythm to gather speed. You're almost like a boxer hitting those rims, and you need precision, strength, and stamina to make it work.

Experienced wheelchair racers say it took them years to master the sport, and I believe it. I was trying to learn it in a few weeks. My main problem was I was holding the rims for too long. A racer needs to strike the rim at twelve o'clock and let go at six o'clock. I kept thinking that I could generate extra power by holding on until eight or nine o'clock, but that just made me go slower. Or sometimes, I'd hit the rim so hard I'd make the wheels flex. Steering around curves was also tricky. The steering wheel is a small triangle, and it just takes a light tap, combined with a body lean, to turn the bike. It's all very subtle, and the slightest error results in a turn that's too wide or too slow or simply out of control. During one practice, I came in like a missile and clipped Coach Skelly.

I thought I could just use my strength to generate speed, but that didn't work. One time, I got so frustrated that I flung the chair in anger. Nonetheless, I had one advantage. Wheelchair racing is all about strength-to-weight ratio—how strong the racer is compared to how much he weighs. In my case, not only had I developed significant strength in my arms and shoulders, but I weighed much less than my peers who had legs. In wheelchair racing, not having lower limbs is mostly an asset. The disadvantage is that legs provide balance and stability in the chair. If I could figure out that part, I'd be able to go fast.

Coach Scott is a big believer in "resistance running"—making training as difficult as possible to build endurance and speed. During practice, he would strap runners in a harness, attach a bungee cord, and then strap the cord to a fence post. Runners would take off and, once they felt resistance, continue pushing, pushing, pushing until they finally snapped back.

So that's what I did, except I was in my chair. Other times, Coach Scott would attach a sled to the back of my bike and put a forty-five-pound weight on it and had me race around the track pulling that heavy weight. I didn't like it, but it made me better. Coach Scott had one of the school's construction trade classes build a stand that allowed me to mount the bike and keep it stationary while I practiced hitting the rims. Coach Scott videotaped these workouts so I could see how I was hanging on to the rim too long.

We practiced Monday through Friday after school, but I needed additional work, so I asked Coach Scott to meet me at the track on Saturday mornings. I know that Coach Scott, who's also Black, was impressed by my commitment. I couldn't drive a car back then, and I refused to take the bus. Because my mom worked long hours, I had to either find a ride to school or push myself in my wheelchair almost three miles. Once I got my racing chair, I couldn't leave it at school because I couldn't risk someone stealing it, so I brought it home each night, attaching it to the back of my regular wheelchair. Coach Scott saw me a couple times, and I guess I was quite the sight: a guy in a wheelchair pulling another wheelchair down the streets of Massillon. He knew I meant business.

When we met on Saturday mornings, he would pick up

me and my bike in his truck, and we'd get to the track; he would stay in the truck and pace me as I tried to keep up. For the record, it's a lot harder to push a wheelchair than to drive a truck. If I didn't keep pace, it wouldn't count as a lap, and we'd be there for a couple hours. By the end of the season, my bike speed was twenty-two miles per hour, which is fast, professionally fast. Sometimes, the girls' track coach, Rachel Adkins, would help—she would run alongside me to make sure I cut my turns properly.

As with wrestling, I had coaches who were willing to do whatever was necessary to help me succeed.

As far as the season went, we had some logistical problems, not least of which was getting my bike to the meets. Citing safety concerns, the school would not allow me to take the bike on the bus, so we had to put the bike on a school van and drive it separately—Coach Scott was always concerned the van would take the bike to the wrong field. Then there were the races themselves. Often, I didn't have any competitors. It is, after all, a specialty sport. On occasion, I'd have someone to race against, in either the one hundred, two hundred, or four hundred meters. Even though I was still a beginner, no one could keep up with me. Most of time, I just raced by myself, though my score didn't count. It was simply an exhibition, which was frustrating. I wasn't some circus performer. I was an elite athlete determined to compete and win.

So I did the next best thing—I competed against myself,

always pushing myself to get a better time. I was also hoping to beat Casey's time in the hundred meters. Casey and I were not true peers, as seated racing has different categories based on functional ability and Casey and I were in different categories. But the state of Ohio combines all seated racers in high school competitions. Casey had graduated the previous year, and regardless of classification, he was the most accomplished seated racer in Ohio history. His time in the hundred meters was 16.97 seconds, and that was the mark I wanted to beat.

Coach Scott and I assumed that I'd be able to compete in the district meet in North Canton—even if I didn't have anyone to compete against, I still wanted to run my race. That's because districts are different from regular meets. The whole community comes out. Classmates. Friends. Relatives. The stands are packed, everyone is hyped, and I wanted to be part of it. But the Ohio High School Athletic Association (OHSAA) said I couldn't participate, claiming the schedule of events was too tight, and it would take too much time to have me run a race.

That was upsetting. OHSAA was telling me that I would go to the state championship by default, without actually racing anyone. But I wanted to earn my way. Then, suddenly, even going to the state championship was in question.

To qualify as a disabled athlete, OHSAA needed a signed medical form confirming my disability, but we were unfamiliar with the rules in track and field, and OHSAA didn't have the medical form as we were approaching the deadline for the state tournament.

Coach Scott called OHSAA and asked for an extension. OHSAA already knew who I was, as two years ago it had given me permission to wrestle from the neutral position. But I guess Coach Scott was dealing with someone else. The organization didn't know me.

"It's Zion Clark," Coach Scott said. "You don't know about him?"

"What condition does he have?" the official asked.

"I don't know!" Coach yelled. "But he doesn't have any legs!"

My mom got the signed paperwork the next day and faxed it over, and we made the deadline.

Someone also started spreading rumors that I had taken steroids, as there seemed no other explanation for how a complete novice could become so good at seated racing so quickly. The state officials never believed it, and the rumor soon died out.

Though I made it to the state championship without actually beating anyone, I was now headed to Columbus. But I had two other milestone events to attend to first.

CHAPTER 20
VICTORY LAPS

I HAD NEVER BEEN to our Homecoming Dance. I had asked girls before, but they had said no. I would tell friends, "That's what I get for not combing my hair." But getting turned down was no fun, particularly when a girl who said no would say yes to another guy. As a senior, I once again couldn't find a date for Homecoming, and I really wanted to go. As mentioned, I spent a lot of time at the Sparkmans' home—Darese was my best friend, Casey was a workout buddy, and their mom and dad were like surrogate parents. There was one other member of the family, Destiny, who was a student at Perry High School.

I asked Darese, "Would you be mad if I asked Des to the prom?"

He said, "Dude, go for it."

So I made a sign that read at the top: "If you go to Homecoming, you will make me jump with joy."

At the bottom it read: "Wait, I don't have legs. Never mind. But will you go with me?"

She said yes.

I wore a pink tuxedo, and she wore a pink dress. I slow-danced in my wheelchair, but for trap music, I was dancing on my hands. In a kind of break dancing, I spun on my back and then spun on my head. I don't do that anymore, but when I was in high school, I was lit.

There were times during my high school years when I doubted that I would graduate from Massillon High School or any high school, so when May 24, 2016, graduation day, came around, I was relieved and elated but mostly proud. And concerned about my long, dark gown. It wasn't made for someone like me, so my mom took it to a seamstress, who not only hemmed it short but used the extra material to create a satchel. The graduation was on the field of our football stadium, and I looked sharp in my tailored gown, my black tie and white shirt, my sunglasses, and my mortar board with orange and black tassel. I wasn't in a wheelchair or wearing prosthetics. I was just walking on my hands, and beneath a bright sun and clear sky, the principal announced my name, adding that I was competing next week in the state championship in track. "Good luck, Zion!"

The crowd erupted. I walked across the field and reached out to shake the principal's hand, and he bent over to hand me my diploma. I then dabbed him and jumped as high as I could. Smiling wide, I put my diploma in my satchel and continued walking. And I heard the cheers.

For my graduation present, I wanted a tattoo, and my mom decided to make it a joint enterprise. We each got one or, well, in my mom's case, more than one. She had the names of her three children tattooed on her arm, and she had a cross tattooed on her chest right above her heart: her faith, the center of her life.

I wanted something bold, something that defined how I had made it this far, and something that would inspire me for the rest of my life. And I had the words tattooed in big letters across my back: **NO EXCUSES**.

I had one more thing to do in high school. Go to state and win a championship.

Massillon had a good track team, boys and girls, and we had a bunch of athletes qualify for the state tournament. We took three different vans down Highway 71 to Columbus. I didn't socialize much on these trips, preferring to sleep or listen to my music. We stayed in a motel and, early the next morning, arrived at the same stadium where Indy had triumphed the year before. I was skittish. This dude named Michael Fenster was considered number one in the state. Now I was going to have to beat him.

We had sixteen wheelchair racers from across Ohio, and in the hundred meters, I blew through the preliminary race that would determine the final eight. For the final, I was in lane three, as the fastest racers go in the middle. As we waited for the gun, I tried to screen out everything around me. My mom and Indy were both in the stands as well as other friends and relatives. So, too, were Lisa, Brett, and Casey Followay, all pulling for me.

The gun sounded. All nervousness left my body; all thoughts emptied from my head. I put all that anxious energy in my forearms, my biceps, my triceps. I struck the rim and exploded off the line, which sent electricity through my fingers. From that very first strike, I was ahead of the field. *Boom. Boom. Boom.* Striking that chair as hard as I could, I didn't want to look back because I didn't want to slow down. Racing was nothing but me and the wind, and I love the feeling of the wind rushing past my ears. I powered through the line and heard Indy screaming for me, which jacked me even more. I looked back and saw the rest of the field breaking the line behind me, and that was my favorite part.

My time was 17.82 seconds, beating Fenster by 0.85 seconds. It was my personal best, though still behind Casey's fastest time. I was finally a champion, bringing home the gold for my school and my family.

I also won the four-hundred-meter race, beating Fenster by only 0.65 seconds. I thought I would take the eight hundred meters as well, but I didn't pace myself and burned out at the end. Trying to go full blast for two minutes and thirty-five seconds, which was my time, was ill advised. I finished third, with Fenster placing first.

I thought I was done, but not yet.

Ohio had one other high school track-and-field sport for

disabled athletes, and that was the shot put. But it required a special mounted chair, in which the seated athlete holds a metal pole with one hand and, using that pole for leverage, flings the metal ball with the other hand. We didn't have that chair in Massillon, but using my regular chair, I would occasionally throw the shot during practice. Our coach showed me how to do it, so I had the right form if not the right equipment, and I could throw the shot about fifteen feet.

Now that we were at state, Coach Scott told me that the right chairs were available, and if I wanted to enter the seated shot put competition, I could.

Why not?

I entered, and I felt pretty comfortable in the chair. Holding the pole with my left hand and leading with my chest, I heaved that sucker three different times, and my best throw—sixteen feet, five inches—put me in second place. Then a freshman from Bowling Green High School, Eric Rine, threw it sixteen feet, ten and three-quarter inches on his final throw and won.

I took third place, which I felt really good about.

When a reporter asked Coach Scott about me, he said, "After coaching Zion, I no longer have any excuses in my life."

Massillon was proud of me. I got to meet the mayor, Kathy Catazaro-Perry, and I was featured in the newspaper and on local broadcasts. The city put up billboards with my picture and even held a Zion Clark Day. It was the ultimate victory lap.

CHAPTER 21

BE A ZION

AS A KID, I once saw a guy who was paralyzed ride a motorcycle (special training wheels were attached), and I also saw a woman who couldn't use her legs drive a car. She hit the gas or the brake by blowing air through a tube. I was twelve or thirteen at the time, and that moment was a revelation. I realized that I would also be able to drive. I didn't know how it would work, but my whole life was about personal innovation, so whatever was needed to drive a car, I would either get that device or develop it myself.

It shouldn't be a surprise that driving was a serious goal of mine—I mean, what teenager doesn't want his own wheels? But whenever I mentioned it to the foster parent I was living with, I was told either that it was too dangerous or that I didn't deserve to drive because I hadn't been a good kid. I always thought it was weird that I was allowed to push my wheelchair up and down the streets of Massillon, where the risk of getting hit was high, but I wasn't able to drive a car.

This was hardly great for my social life. By the time you're sixteen, you want to be able to pick up your date in a car, even if you're stuck in your parents' jalopy or, worse, a minivan. But I could never do that. Or a girl would pick me up in her car, and I'd have to shove my wheelchair in the trunk. Not ideal.

Everything changed after I moved in with my mom. She never put limits on me, so when I told her I wanted to learn how to drive, she investigated how to make it happen, and when I was nineteen, she bought me a used Dodge Caliber. It was silver and honestly not the sleekest car on the road, but it had hand controls—my thumb controlled the gas, a hand lever applied the brakes. My mom taught me the rules of the road, and I got my license.

It was great to finally have the independence of having a car, and I could do the basic maintenance—I pump my own gas, for example, as my arms are long enough to handle all the logistics. In 2021, I upgraded and bought a white Honda Civic Hatchback.

After high school, I attended two small colleges in Ohio, Stark State College for a semester and then Kent State University at Tuscarawas in New Philadelphia, which is about twenty-five miles south of Massillon. I wrestled at both schools and discovered that college wrestling is nothing like high school wrestling—the practices are more grueling, the competition much tougher. Each match is still three periods, but the first is three minutes instead of two. That one minute is a big difference.

By the time I enrolled at Kent State, in the fall of 2017, I had continued to bulk up and weighed close to one hundred pounds, but I was still significantly underweight. The lowest weight class in college is 125 pounds, so I was more underweight than I had been in high school. I also had to begin the second or third periods in the top or bottom position, negating the neutral position rule we secured in high school. But I took on all comers. One on occasion, Kent State's wrestler at 133 pounds dropped out in a dual meet against Lackawanna College. I volunteered to go up a weight class and beat Yahnzy Ortiz, 6–4.

I still hated to lose any match, but even more disappointing was that during that 2017 season, five of my opponents forfeited because they didn't want to wrestle someone without legs. It's one thing to forfeit if you're in middle school or high school, but college? You're a grown man. Act like it. One opposing coach told my coach, Dave Schlarb, that his wrestler forfeited because losing to me would have been too demoralizing.

Kent State is a member of the USCAA (United States Collegiate Athletic Association), which consists of mostly small colleges. I qualified for nationals and was seeded sixteenth for the tournament. I won in a few upsets and finished sixth. I won thirteen matches for the year, and I think

I surprised a lot of people with how well I did in my first full collegiate season.

I was also an attraction. I didn't even notice it, because I was so focused on my opponents, but my roommate, Austin Bailey, later told me that win or lose, I would always get a standing ovation. I had already received a lot of local media attention, and ESPN had done a segment on me in high school, but in August 2018, Netflix released an eleven-minute documentary on me. Suddenly, I was receiving emails, text messages, and calls from strangers all over the United States and from other countries. Then in May 2019, Ellen DeGeneres invited my mom and me on her show. We flew out to Los Angeles, and at the end of the segment, Ellen said she had something for my mom.

A divider onstage opened, revealing a Chevy Traverse. We walked over to it, and above the cheering crowd, Ellen said, "This 2019 Chevy Traverse is ready for anything. It has the technology to keep you on track, and all the space you need. It's yours!"

My mom, in disbelief, screamed, "Oh, my God!"

The Lord works in mysterious ways.

I enjoyed all the attention, and it made me realize that I had other opportunities. But I was still at Kent State. I liked Coach Schlarb and the school, but it was not lost on me that Kent State was selling wrestling shirts for profit but not sharing those profits with the wrestlers themselves while also denying us the ability to sell our name or likeness. The system was unjust for all college athletes, but I was now getting offers for endorsements and speaking engagements. (In a 2021 ruling, the US Supreme Court allowed a loosening of restrictions against college athletes receiving compensation from companies.)

My second year at Kent State, I was still on the wrestling team, but I missed a chunk of time to attend a family funeral in Georgia, and I wasn't focused academically. I felt I had other opportunities, and they weren't at school. My grades lagged, and I lost my eligibility to compete in matches. I mainly regret that I'll never know how far I could have gone in my second full year, but I knew that other doors were opening for me.

In March 2019, while still at Kent State, I was invited to compete in the annual Arnold Classic in Columbus, founded by Arnold Schwarzenegger and featuring bodybuilding and calisthenic events, including those for disabled athletes. I went to Columbus with Michaela Marcelli, a friend of mine from Massillon who would sometimes help me on my trips. She understood me better than most, in part because her father, Cork Marcelli, was not only a high school wrestling coach but had been raised in foster homes in Akron and had used sports as a ticket out of a difficult childhood.

Michaela herself is a very good athlete—she played softball in high school—and was in the crowd when I wrestled in districts against Jack Gorman. She was convinced that even Gorman, in his own way, was kind of on my side.

"You could tell he didn't feel good about beating you," Michaela told me.

I'm not sure about that, but it was nice of her to say.

When Michaela and I headed to Columbus for the Arnold Classic, we had no idea how big it was. It drew more than twenty-two thousand athletes to compete in eighty events, while drawing about two hundred thousand fans. The big hotels were all booked, so Michaela and I ended up at some dinky motel, which only had one small room for two people.

When we walked inside, Michaela quipped, "Too bad they didn't have a one-and-a-half-sized room."

I laughed. I love talking trash with my friends and don't take offense to anyone making light of my disability—as long as I know the words are spoken out of respect and friendship. Besides, if you can't laugh about things with your friends, you'll go crazy. I poke fun at myself all the time.

I made a funny remark about Michaela's unruly hair, and we made the best out of our cramped living quarters.

The actual event was exciting, in part because the emcee for our competition was Nick Scott, who's a legend among disabled athletes. In 1998, when he was sixteen years old, he was driving his 1984 Buick Skylark in Pomona, Kansas, when the left front tire blew out. The car careened into a ditch, rolled five and a half times, and ejected Nick from the driver's seat. The vehicle literally hit him in the back as he was flung to the ground. The accident left him paralyzed from the waist down and in a wheelchair. One moment, he was a high school football player dreaming of glory on the gridiron. The next moment, he was told he would never walk again. Returning to school only deepened his depression, as it reminded him of the life he once had. Overweight and isolated, he all but gave up on life and could have easily been a permanent victim of a terrible accident.

But he took a different route, putting himself through a grueling physical rehabilitation effort, over several years, to rebuild his body. He could never play football again, but that didn't destroy his competitive spirit. He became a dedicated power lifter and was determined to beat able-bodied lifters. His strength blossomed, his confidence grew, and he began winning power-lifting competitions. He was also committed to walking again. When he graduated from high school, he used crutches to walk across the stage, which was a major achievement. But he continued working on the treadmill, training his legs, practicing, one foot in front of the other.

When Nick graduated from Ottawa University in Kansas in 2005, he walked, gingerly but triumphantly, across the stage with his diploma.

And he was just getting started. Since he was lifting

weights, Nick figured he'd become a bodybuilder—Schwarzenegger in a wheelchair. It was a brazen act of defiance. His body, seemingly damaged beyond repair, had been a source of shame. Nick transformed it into a source of chiseled pride.

He entered more than 250 wheelchair bodybuilding events around the world and won several championships. He also excelled at wheelchair ballroom dancing—he's in a wheelchair; his partner is not—and he and Aubree Marchione became the first couple in history to represent the United States at the World International Paralympic Committee Wheelchair Dance Sport Championships in Hannover, Germany.

Nick realized the power of his story and became a motivational speaker and celebrity. His message is all about turning self-pity into opportunity, or as he likes to say, "My disability became a possibility."

I never saw my life quite like Nick did, as I didn't have that life-altering event to overcome. I was simply born this way. But Nick is still a role model for anyone who faces adversity or for anyone who feels so overwhelmed, they are just ready to give up.

We had a couple of phone calls, before and after the Arnold Classic, and I asked Nick what made him different. He says that to be successful, we all need a "why factor." Why do you do what you do? Nick says his "why factor" is his mother,

Sylvia Scott, who after his accident was there by his side in the hospital and never gave up on him. He was determined to win trophies for her, to walk for her, to make her proud.

That makes sense to me. I think every kid needs that unconditional love from a parent, regardless of whether that kid has a disability. It's no coincidence that I only began to get my life in order once Miss Kim adopted me and I experienced that unconditional love for the first time.

The Arnold Classic was held before thousands of screaming fans at the Greater Columbus Convention Center. I had never participated in a calisthenics competition, and I was competing against two other inspiring athletes. There was Woody Belfort, a lean but muscular bodybuilder from Canada whose cerebral palsy limits his ability to use his legs and usually uses a wheelchair; and Zach Ruhl, a muscle-bound, tattooed bodybuilder from Texas who had both legs amputated at age two due to a rare bone condition. Even though this was a competition for a medal, we were all cheering each other on, and with the music pumped up and Nick exhorting us from the stage and the crowd going bonkers, the atmosphere was supercharged. Woody's routine included handstand push-ups using only *one finger*. Zach, while strapped into his wheelchair, flung himself around the pull-up bar even though he had broken an elbow before the competition.

Doing calisthenics to build body strength is one thing, but doing them to entertain a crowd is something else entirely. As it happens, just a couple of months before the Arnold, I was at wrestling practice, and my teammates were doing backflips. I wanted to do a backflip also but was afraid that I would land wrong and hurt my neck. I needed someone to pump me up, so I had my good friend and teammate Austin Bailey slap me in the face as hard as he could. It worked: it jolted me, and I did four consecutive backflips.

I would incorporate those into my Arnold Classic routine, but I still didn't have anything mapped out. I was going to improvise.

Nick, in his black dress shirt and black tie, introduced me to the audience. "Since his mother gave him up for adoption, he's lived in seven or eight different foster homes . . . and so at times growing up, he was starved, he was beaten, and he was bullied a lot. . . . He competes at 125-pound class at Kent State University. . . . Right now, welcome Zion Clark, known as Jaws!"

Jaws was a nickname that my college teammates gave me because my grip was so tight.

Whereas Woody and Zach began their routines in their wheelchairs, and Zach stayed in his chair, I didn't use a wheelchair at all. I was just on my hands, and after Nick's introduction, I took off my shirt and showed off my muscles. I had sixty seconds to do a routine, and then I'd have two more rounds of sixty seconds. The only requirement was to impress Nick and the audience.

I jumped on a couple of wooden boxes and did a handstand, first using two hands and then just one. The big video screen showed the **NO EXCUSES** tattoo on my back.

"Let's hear it for Zion!" Nick bellowed.

I walked over to the high bar, and Nick yelled, "Let's see some tricks! They want to see what you got, Zion!"

I did five pull-ups on the high bar and then dismounted with a backflip.

I then did one more backflip, and Nick said, "Give it up for Zion!"

Next round, I once again did a handstand on the boxes, but this time added three clap push-ups.

That wasn't good enough for Nick, who yelled, "Let's see some one-handed upside-down push-ups!"

So, while back on the ground, I did a handstand, then lifted my left arm and, with my left hand, reached back and grabbed the bottom of my shorts, to give me maximum verticality. I then did several one-handed push-ups.

"That's a legendary move right there!" Nick yelled.

For my last round, I went back to the high bar and did a one-arm handstand, then I ran the gauntlet of four wooden boxes—jumping from one to the next.

For the grand finale, and completely unplanned, Woody, Zach, and I took center stage, and with Woody and Zach in their wheelchairs, I climbed up on their backs, put one hand on each of their shoulders, and did a handstand.

It was a benign freak show—the three of us doing physical stunts that were beyond the comprehension of anyone in the audience.

To determine the winner, Nick asked the fans to cheer for their favorite performer. I don't think they wanted that responsibility—they gave each of us loud ovations, in genuine appreciation. Nick deemed Woody the winner and gave me second place, but, man, we were all winners.

Unfortunately, I injured my left hand on one of my dismounts and eventually found out that I'd fractured a bone. Not only did I complete my routines but I also entered a pull-up contest sponsored by the US Marines. It was open to everyone, and despite my broken hand, I still did thirty-five pull-ups and snared first place.

Meanwhile, I loved hanging out backstage and meeting other athletes from all over the world, and I didn't mind the attention from female bodybuilders, some of whom asked if they could rub me down with body oil. Who was I to say no?

The Arnold Classic opened my eyes to what I could be. As an athlete, I had always competed with one purpose—to win—and that was the only way to measure performance. But at the Arnold Classic, no one cared who won. We were there to entertain and to inspire and to demonstrate to the world that people in wheelchairs will not be limited.

I still wanted to compete as an athlete and win, but I was beginning to realize that there were other ways to measure success.

One day during my second year at Kent State, the athletic director, Robert Brindley, came into my class and asked me to see him in his office. I feared I had done something wrong and was now going to pay the price.

Once I got to his office, Mr. Brindley put down a stack of papers, and I immediately thought: *I've done something wrong, and here is the evidence against me.* Instead, Mr. Brindley said, "You have to read these."

They were letters written by children at Elizabeth Price Elementary School in Cuyahoga Falls. They had seen the Netflix documentary and wanted to reach out to me. Mr. Brindley said many of these students were refugees from Syria. They had escaped the war. In some cases, their families were killed. These children were survivors.

I brought the letters back to my apartment and read each one two or three times. Some of the kids talked about their struggles in school, or their siblings, or just being different. One letter had a drawing of me and the message "Be a Zion."

It practically brought me to tears.

I went back to Mr. Brindley and asked if there was something we could do for these children. He said he'd look into it.

He arranged for me to visit Price Elementary and speak

to the students. I'm guessing I spoke to about a hundred kids, and this was a new experience. I had been interviewed before, and that was easy—just answer the questions. But that's different from standing in front of an audience, all eyes on you, and talking without any prompts. The age of the audience didn't matter. I was nervous. I think they were nervous, too, seeing someone like me. It didn't make me any less nervous when Fox 8 News showed up to film me.

I just started talking about my life. I don't know what it's like to be a refugee, but I do know what it's like to be abandoned. I told the kids that we all face challenges, we all face setbacks, and when that happens, "you can either stand your ground and do something, or you can back away. I chose not to back away."

Soon enough, all the nervousness left the room and was replaced by smiles—mine and theirs. It felt like Christmas.

One student, fourth grader Saurab Dhakal, told Fox 8 News: "Life is always a struggle, and nothing can come easy without hard work. [Zion] made me feel like I could do anything in the world."

My presentation had one more twist.

I called the girl up who had written "Be a Zion" on her letter, and I said to her, "I've got a surprise for you and for everyone here."

I then opened a box and lifted a T-shirt inscribed—in the

girl's handwriting—"Be a Zion." The shirt also had the picture that she had drawn on the letter.

Kent State, with the help of BSN Sports, a sportswear company, had created the T-shirts by photographing the girl's letter and transferring it onto the material. The shirt also had Kent State's colors, blue and gold.

"Do you remember drawing this picture?" I asked her.

She said yes, but she couldn't believe her drawing and her inscription had made their way onto a shirt and that the shirts would now be distributed to everyone there. I'm not sure I could believe it, either.

It was one of the most moving experiences in my life. For so long, I thought no one would listen to me or believe me or care what I had to say. I had a story but didn't believe I was capable of sharing it or was even worthy of sharing it. I thought people saw me for what I didn't have—parents, a home, legs—instead of what I did have.

Those kids from Price Elementary, refugees from Syria, opened my eyes.

BE A ZION.

CHAPTER 22
TRIALS AND TRIBULATIONS

JUST AS I continued wrestling after high school, so, too, with seated racing. Three weeks after I won the state championship, I traveled to Wisconsin for the Junior Nationals, which are a weeklong competition for disabled athletes. I won the hundred meters. Afterward, a representative of Team USA asked me how long I'd been racing.

"Three months," I told him.

He didn't believe it.

Team USA consists of Olympic and Paralympic athletes, and the following year, the organization began inviting me to its meets. I was now competing against high-level professionals who were among the best in the world. Though I wasn't winning any races, I was beating more experienced competitors and slowly climbing in the rankings. I set my sights on making the USA Paralympic team for the Tokyo games in 2020, and then, after they were postponed, for 2021.

I was a long shot, as I'd be competing against guys who'd been racing for ten, fifteen, twenty years. But each year I was improving, and I thought I had a good chance of making the team.

Early in 2021, I moved to San Diego to train. The weather there is ideal, and I was also involved in a start-up business located there. I was living, on a temporary basis, in a dingy La Quinta motel, and each morning I drove to the open-air Self Made Training Facility Mission Bay, right next to a doggie day care center. At this point, I could lift more than three hundred pounds without anyone holding me to the bench. Beneath a big poster of Arnold Schwarzenegger and flags that read "Don't Tread on Me," and with the dogs barking in their play area, I pushed myself until my body gave out: stretching thick bands for resistance training, lifting barbells for strength, riding the stationary bike for endurance.

I then drove to Point Loma Nazarene University, whose empty track looks over the Pacific Ocean. As Coach Donahue taught us, **CHAMPIONS ARE MADE WHEN NO ONE IS WATCHING,** and there were plenty of days that I went to the track and no one was watching.

One day at the track, I began to assemble my custom-made six-thousand-dollar lightweight-carbon wheelchair racing bike, but I realized I was missing a bolt that attaches a wheel to the bike. If I couldn't find the bolt, I'd have to order it from a company in Florida, and it would take ten days to arrive. But I didn't have ten days. I was leaving in five days for Mesa, Arizona, where the Desert Challenge Games 2021 would determine which Americans qualified for the Paralympic trials the following month in Minneapolis.

That's the life of a disabled athlete. You could spend two years preparing for a Paralympic trial, and then a missing bolt could dash your dreams.

I found the bolt. It had fallen out of my bike bag the day before and sat on the ground overnight.

I attached my wheels, put on my blood-flecked gloves, and with the sun beating down, began my workout, sprinting for one hundred meters, then coasting. Sprinting, coasting. Sprint. Coast. Sprint. Coast.

Until my heart raced and sweat poured down my face.

I had lifted weights so intensely in recent years that I had bulked up to 125 pounds—I had stretch marks across my biceps. But now I needed to lose weight. So after each workout, I would drive back to the motel and turn on the shower full blast, scalding hot, place towels beneath the door, sit on the covered toilet, and in the steaming, sweltering bathroom, envision victory in Tokyo. For dinner I'd have a salad, as I'd eliminated fast food, junk food, candy, and alcohol. I lost twenty-five pounds with this regimen, and before I went to bed, I'd watch videos of the top wheelchair racers in the world and get ready to repeat the day's routine tomorrow.

I thought I was prepared for the Desert Challenge Games in May, but the meet was a disaster. Though I had been training, I hadn't actually competed in well over a year, and I was rusty. During my four-hundred-meter race, the ratchet strap on the back of my chair broke. The chair wobbled, and I crashed while traveling close to twenty miles per hour. My head hit the pavement three times as I went sprawling. I had muscle spasms and couldn't feel my back. An ambulance took me to the hospital, but I had nothing worse than bruises. The following day, I competed in the hundred-meter race, and this time my compensator, which reduces the vibrations on the steering mechanism, broke. I finished eleventh out of eighteen.

Somewhat bruised and battered, I competed the following week in Chula Vista, near San Diego, and qualified for the hundred-meter trials in June in Minnesota, where the top two racers would make the Paralympic team.

In the years before the pandemic, I had consistently finished behind Erik Hightower, who'd already competed in two Paralympics and finished seventh in the hundred-meter at the Rio de Janeiro games in 2016. Erik was in his thirties and would always chat with me before and after races. He couldn't have been nicer, which didn't mean anything once the race began. I thought I could win the race if I beat Erik, and even if I got second place, I'd still make the team.

The trials were at Breck School in Golden Valley, a suburb of Minneapolis. I didn't have to push myself in the preliminaries, as the top four made it to the finals. I cruised and finished third. The next day, the finals, was sunny and hot, with the stands virtually empty because of the pandemic. As I waited for our late-afternoon race, I wrapped a cold towel around my neck, flipped on my headphones, and meditated. We were finally called to the line, and I knew that I'd have to run my best race ever to make the team.

Well, I did run my best race ever—15.29 seconds—but I was behind from the beginning and finished fourth. I was a full 1.05 seconds behind the winner, which in a hundred-meter race isn't that close. What surprised me was that Erik only got second. He was behind a twenty-three-year-old named Daniel Romanchuk, who had previously raced in marathons and won them, but now was also a sprinter. Both Daniel and Erik made Team USA.

I certainly wanted to be on that team, but I wasn't disappointed in myself, not at all. I was actually pretty excited. Daniel and I are the same age, but he'd been racing since he was six years old. Erik began racing when he was eight. I started at eighteen—and I was still the fourth best in the country.

After the race, Daniel rode up to me and said, "Hey, dude, that was a cool race."

"Yeah, you're fast," I told him.

"You're fast, too," he said.

We'll cross paths again. Same with Erik.

The 2024 Paralympics are in Paris.

CHAPTER 23
YOUNG VOICES RISING

I'M A BLACK MAN in America, and I'm reminded of that all the time.

In 2020, I was visiting a friend in San Diego, just chilling, and around three in the morning, I got in my wheelchair and rolled down to the Chevron station, which had a mini-mart. I went inside to buy a pack of Swishers cigars, and a white cop came up to me as I was leaving.

"Come talk to me for a second," he said.

I was wearing a black hoodie, so maybe I looked suspicious.

"What are you doing here?" he asked.

"I just bought a pack of Swishers."

"Well, people have been getting robbed around here. I hope it's not you doing it. Can you answer some questions?"

"Man, I don't even live out here. I just want to get back to my friend's house. Let me go. Please."

He said no. He needed to question me. So he went through his questions. He asked me if I'd been around Bank of America's ATMs in downtown San Diego and if I used Bank of America as my main bank.

"No, man!" I said. "I use Fifth Third."

"What's that?"

I told him it was a bank in Ohio.

He never accused me of anything. He just kept asking me questions. He finally asked me for my ID, which I gave him.

"Oh," he said. "I see you're from Ohio."

"That's what I've been trying to tell you!"

He told me to have a good night.

Those kinds of encounters, multiplied by tens of thousands, are why so many young Black people are demanding change, and I want to be part of that change.

After George Floyd's murder, I delivered a message on Instagram that said everyone needs to "keep their head up . . . keep on grinding . . . keep believing in yourself . . . because when this is all said and done, we'll have to get back to our normal lives, and when we do that, we still have to support ourselves, our families, everybody." That post alone received thirty-four thousand views.

When the Black Lives Matter movement protests gathered steam in the summer of 2020, my friends nominated me as one of its leaders. While it was just a title—I had no responsibilities—I gladly accepted. I believe I'm respected by a broad spectrum of people: thugs and athletes, business executives and religious leaders. I've been part of all of their worlds.

I know what it's like to be angry—and not just angry but raging-mad angry. I've been called all the names, and I'm still a target. After I appeared on *The Ellen DeGeneres Show*, I received messages of love and support from all over the world, but I also received death threats. And they still come, hundreds of messages of hate, from trolls hoping to provoke me.

They don't like it when a Black man succeeds, particularly a young Black man, particularly someone in my condition. I mean, look at me. One hundred years ago, America had a thriving eugenics movement—the belief that certain populations were genetically inferior. And who might these undesirables be?

Poor people.

People of color.

The disabled.

Check. Check. Check.

Immigrants and folks with mental illnesses were also targeted, and these eugenicists were ruthless. During the twentieth century, thirty-two states implemented federally funded sterilization programs to limit the spread of undesirables, also known as "degenerate stock." In upholding one such law, US Supreme Court Justice Oliver Wendell Holmes in 1927 famously wrote: "Three generations of imbeciles are enough."

I wasn't born into that world, but it's naive to believe that our attitudes toward the disabled are any more evolved than our attitudes toward people of color. I also think my disability put an even bigger chip on my shoulder regarding race. When I was younger, if someone made a racist taunt, I'd swing at him. That happened plenty of times. It's worth noting that the state of Ohio has a long, sad history as a stronghold for the Ku Klux Klan. During the Klan's heyday in the 1920s, the city of Dayton was a hub, and Klan-affiliated groups are still holding rallies in Dayton and across the state.

If you're Black, it doesn't matter if you're old or young, rich or poor. The threat against you is there.

The Black Lives Matter protests are about a lot more than police brutality. They're about the frustration of young Black people who can't get ahead in this country. We can't afford college, we can't find jobs, we can't pay rent, we can't get out of our communities. We may have the same rights that white people have—and slavery may be over, lynchings may be over, Jim Crow may be over—but we're still stuck. And we've been stuck for a long time. I felt stuck for a long time. I know first-hand the pressure, anger, frustration, and pain that builds and builds until some trigger ignites an explosion.

But we don't need violence. When I visit schools and talk to kids, I make it simple: If you poke me in my hand, I'll bleed red. If I poke you in your hand, you'll bleed red. We're all the same; we're all in this together. Now we just have to work together to make a better world.

I realize the world is much more complicated than that, but if the adults can't figure it out, maybe the kids can.

If our racial problems have been well known for a long time, the same cannot be said about our failed foster care system. That's why when I decided to write this book in 2020, I did so in part to bring attention to that failure in Ohio and across the country. The media, I thought, had not done enough so that when foster kids spoke out about the system, they were often ignored.

But some failures cannot be overlooked forever.

In October 2020, *USA Today* ran a lengthy investigative story about Florida's foster care system and documented the widespread abuse of children. As the headline said, "Florida Took Thousands of Kids from Families, Then Failed to Keep Them Safe." Then in April 2021, another tragedy occurred that hit closer to home. The police shot and killed a Black teenager, Ma'Khia Bryant, in Columbus, Ohio, while Bryant was lunging at a woman with a steak knife. Bryant and her sister, Ja'Niah, were both in foster care—Ma'Khia had had five placements in two years. Three weeks before Ma'Khia was killed, her sister called 911 and told the dispatcher, "I want to leave this foster home. I want to leave this foster home."

Ma'Khia's death received extensive coverage, much of it centered on, as the *New York Times* wrote, her "turbulent journey through the foster care system" and how it "failed her in critical ways."

The coverage is overdue, and most of the recommendations on improving foster care are sound: more resources for preparing the foster parents themselves while also ensuring that they are fit for the job, and more resources for additional caseworkers and their training. The foster kids themselves need services for their physical, mental, and emotional health. Making the recommendations are easy, however. Making them a reality is another story. That won't happen until we have leaders who put the interests of children first—not just the children of intact families or the children of wealth and privilege, but the children who are abandoned, dispossessed, or unwanted.

Even the discussions on improving foster care leave out many of those kids. In the spring of 2021, I watched Jake Tapper on CNN interview Patricia Babcock, the former deputy assistant secretary for the Florida Department of Children and Families. She said to improve the foster care system, we need to improve the original home environment of those foster children—intervene before they must be moved into foster care. And once that removal occurs, we need to assist the "kinship family" so that child can return.

"I think there's very few children," she said, "who would not fare better back in their home."

But for those children who never had a home, where are they to go?

We don't have an answer for that. All I know is that when we are talking about racial discrimination or foster care abuses or most anything else—climate, education, crime—young people are affected directly. They should have a voice. And they should be listened to.

EPILOGUE
WORK WITH WHAT YOU GOT

THE MOST IMPORTANT PEOPLE in my life remain so.

Granny lives in the same house in Canton. She is now in her late eighties, and with two hip replacements, arthritis, and back problems, she can't go to church anymore. But she is a spiritual anchor of her community, her small home still welcoming me and all others. So much of what she has experienced—all the denigration and disrespect—could have destroyed her, but her faith won out.

I once asked her what's kept her going all these years, and she said, "When I was a little girl, I used to lay on a cotton sheet and look up and wonder what was up there. I couldn't see anything, but in my mind as a little kid, there had to be something up there. And then when I got grown and read the Bible, and read about heaven and earth, and who made it and who separated it, I just knew."

In me, I think, she sees the fulfillment of her faith. She tells me about the time when I was living with her and I came down the stairs and said, "I don't care where I go or who I be with. I ain't never going to forget you."

Granny beams when she tells me that story. "That made me feel so good!" she tells me. "I wanted you to fly."

So, too, did the Schmuckers. Unfortunately, Mr. Schmucker passed away in 2019, but Mrs. Schmucker still lives on the same quiet street in Louisville. She now has one child in the house, a Black youth who is disabled and whom she adopted.

She and her husband were always my biggest advocates. She once said to me, "One day, you're going to be an ambassador."

"What's that?" I asked.

"Someone who can show the world that you can be anything you want to be."

My mom, of course, made everything possible. She is no longer a foster parent but offers respite services to other foster children. She is also finding new ways to affirm her faith. She saw a video of the northern lights, and, seeking the best view possible, she traveled by herself to Iceland, Ireland, and England in the summer of 2021. That's a long way to glimpse the northern lights, but as she tells me, "The Good Book says that the sky declares God's glory."

▪ ▪ ▪

Several months after I graduated from high school, on a rainy day in October 2016, I waited for a bus to meet some friends at the Belden Village Mall in North Canton. When I got on and took my seat, a Black woman next to me looked over and said, "Are you Zion Daniels?"

That was my surname at birth but not a name that I had used in many years.

"Excuse me," I said. "How do you know what my name is?"

"I'm your mother," she said.

She had my facial features. I could see the resemblance.

I was nineteen and had never spoken to, seen, or heard from her. Over the years, I had asked my caseworkers and foster parents about her and how I might reach her, but I never got an answer. Suddenly, here she was, right next to me, on a random bus headed to North Canton.

She told me that she'd been looking for me, which I didn't believe. My picture had been on billboards, and the local newspaper and television stations had done stories on me. I mean, I had been on ESPN. How hard could I be to find? She kept talking, and now that I had made something of myself, she seemed to think we could patch things up and move forward. But I asked her questions that had long been on my mind.

Why she did she give me up? Why didn't she ever come and see me? Why didn't she take better care of herself?

She just shrugged. She wanted to talk about the future. I wanted to talk about the past. And my anger began to rise.

The bus rolled along Everhard Road, and I simmered until I couldn't stand being next to her anymore. The bus came to a stop, and though we were two full stops before the mall and light rain was falling, I hopped off my seat, walked to the door, and jumped out. The last thing I said to her was "Don't talk to me."

I haven't heard from her since.

There was one other thing that I noticed. Her diabetes had apparently taken a toll on her health. She was missing a leg.

Now that I'm an adult, it's much easier for me to stay in touch with my biological brother, Samuel, and I don't take that for granted. By 2021, his mother, Shannon, had married, so Samuel now has a father and is growing up in a stable, loving family. Over the Fourth of July holiday, I went to visit him in Ohio, and we had a cookout at my mom's house, visited Kelcey, got ice cream, and went to Dave & Buster's and played video games. Beyond our physical similarities, he taps on stuff like I do; when he's bored, he puts his head in his arms like I do; he makes the same facial expressions. He is just now, at fifteen, beginning to grow into his body. He is also intelligent, and he wants to play sports. We are unmistakably brothers, and he means the world to me. When I said goodbye, I told him, "Even if I don't see you, remember that I'm your brother, and I love you."

We now play video games remotely, and he usually wins.

The most important contribution I can make is to serve as a role model for people of all races, abilities, and backgrounds, but particularly young people. I hear from them all the time, in the gym, on social media, or wherever I'm invited to speak. Invariably, they ask me the same question: How did you do it?

I tell them that what I did is what anyone can do. Are you feeling like the world is against you, like you're flat on your back? Well, you can't get any lower, so why not dust yourself off and get up? Show strength not for someone else's gratification but for yourself. You may be in a terrible place, but you can work every day to get out of that place, one step at a time—and remember that no hardship can destroy your dreams.

I tell the children and young adults I meet that you don't have to be an athlete. You can be a scientist, a teacher, an artist. You can be a volunteer, a coach, a friend. You just have to find your passion and pursue it. But no one is going to do it for you. If I can do it, so can you.

I'm trying to be the best man I can be, and one day I want to be the best father I can be. And long after I'm dead, I want my children and grandchildren to talk about me as someone who did what no one thought possible, someone who worked with the gifts that God gave him, someone who tried to make life better for family and friends, and someone who changed the world.

WORK WITH WHAT YOU GOT!